Tessellation Quilts

Sensational designs from interlocking patterns

Christine Porter

Photography by Neil Porter

David and Charles

Dedication

To my mother, Muriel Rosenthal and my grandmother,
Grace Munt, who both taught me to sew – two wonderful
women who inspired me throughout their lives.

A DAVID & CHARLES BOOK
Copyright © David & Charles Limited 2006

David & Charles is an F+W Publications Inc. company
4700 East Galbraith Road
Cincinnati, OH 45236

First published in the UK in 2006

Text and designs copyright © Christine Porter 2006

Christine Porter has asserted her right to be identified as author of this work
in accordance with the Copyright, Designs and Patents Act, 1988.

All quilts have been made by Christine Porter unless otherwise stated.

A catalogue record for this book is available from the British Library.

ISBN-13: 978-0-7153-2456-1 hardback
ISBN-10: 0-7153-2456-X hardback

ISBN-13: 978-0-7153-1941-3 paperback (USA only)
ISBN-10: 0-7153-1941-8 paperback (USA only)

Printed in China by SNP Leefung
for David & Charles
Brunel House   Newton Abbot   Devon

Executive Editor   Cheryl Brown
Editor   Ame Verso
Project Editor   Betsy Hosegood
Technical Reader   Dianne Huck
Head of Design   Prudence Rogers
Designer   Jodie Lystor
Production Controller   Ros Napper

Visit our website at **www.davidandcharles.co.uk**

David & Charles books are available from all good bookshops; alternatively you can contact our Orderline
on 0870 9908222 or write to us at FREEPOST EX2 110, D&C Direct, Newton Abbot, TQ12 4ZZ (no stamp
required UK only); US customers call 800-289-0963 and Canadian customers call 800-840-5220.

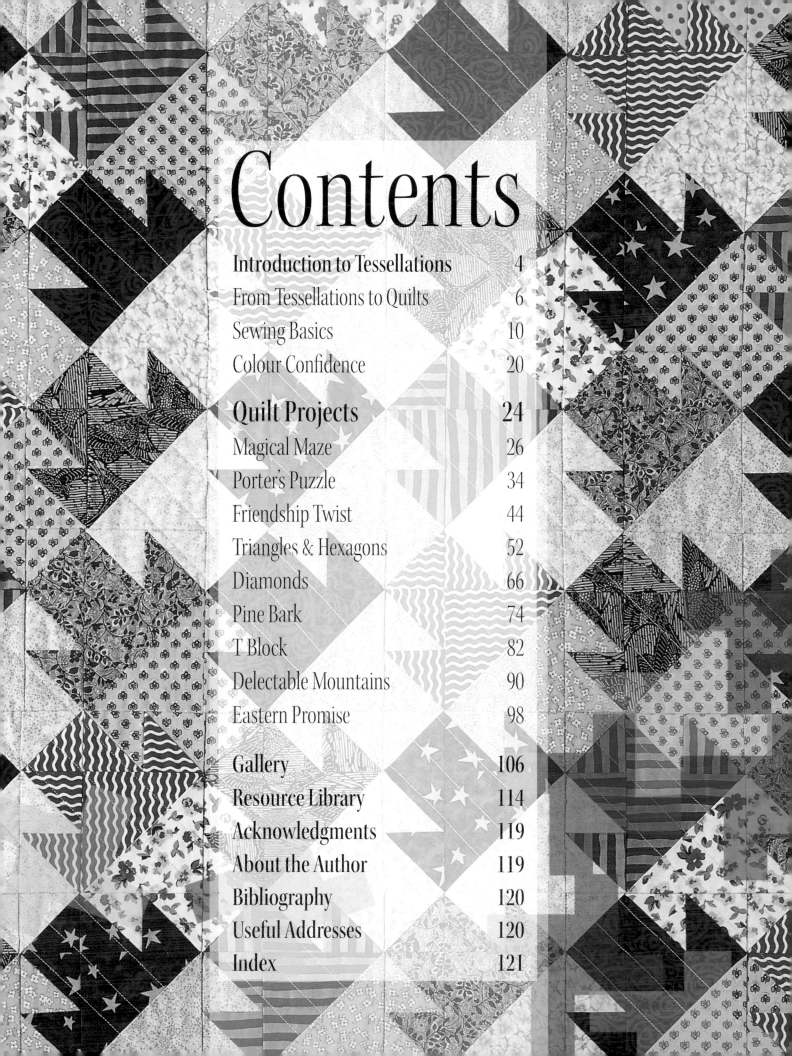

Contents

Introduction to Tessellations

A tessellated pattern is one that interlocks, creating identical positive and negative spaces that can go on indefinitely. It is of particular interest to the quilter because once pieced together the design often looks like a quilting impossibility and it takes time to work out how it was done. If you read through this book you'll find many examples that stop you in your tracks and keep you guessing, rather like a clever conjurer's trick.

Snail's Trail is a popular tessellating pattern that looks complicated but is actually built up in square blocks. Porter's Puzzle (see page 34) is a similar design that was actually inspired by a dogtooth check fabric.

Tumbling Blocks is a familiar tessellation that creates a seemingly three-dimensional design through the careful placement of light, medium and dark toned fabrics.

In this book I wanted to do more than just show you a selection of tessellating designs for you to copy. I wanted to help you use your own creative flair to transform them and even lead you on the path to designing your own tessellations. With this in mind I have designed several variations of each of the nine main quilts so you can get an idea of just what can be achieved.

Once you have read the instructions and can see how the quilts are assembled, you should be able to create your own variations. In fact, when I teach a class I am always interested to see how individuals using the same pattern can end up making quilts that look entirely different from each other, and I am confident that you can take the designs in this book and interpret them in your own way.

I used tessellating patterns from Italian floor tiles here, interpreting the marbled tiles using batik fabrics.

Designed by bees and re-created by man, the honeycomb is not only an interesting tessellation, but is also strong enough to support the massive biomes of the Eden Project, Cornwall, UK.

Nature surprises us with its clever ingenuity at every turn and is a source of some fascinating tessellations, including the hexagonal design of the honeycomb.

You don't have to look far to find examples of tessellations. They are all around us and it has been fun exploring possibilities outside the traditional patterns we already know in patchwork such as Snail's Trail (left, top) and Tumbling Blocks (left, bottom). In fact, it was while enjoying my other great passion, gardening, that I came across an extraordinary example of Tumbling Blocks straight from nature. We have beehives in our garden and it dawned on me that the shapes of the honeycombs were exact hexagons (centre right). When I visited the Eden Project in Cornwall I saw the design again, this time in the construction of the biomes (top right).

I have included an example of a hexagonal design in this book (Beverley Mosaics, page 53), which is made up of six triangles rather than the more usual three diamonds of the Tumbling Blocks design. A variation of that design can be found on floor tiles in Venice where the top diamond has been split into three colours to create a three-dimensional effect. I used this design in my quilt Venetian Inspiration (detail shown above).

Floor tiles hold a fascination for me (see my earlier book, *Quilt Designs from Decorative Floor Tiles*), and these often provide examples of tessellated patterns that are inspirational for the quilter. Many patios and drives are made of tessellating tile patterns (see the brick pattern below) and once you start noticing them you'll begin to see them everywhere, as I do.

You can find examples of tessellating patterns in ordinary bricks and wall tiles.

5

From Tessellations to Quilts

Just how can a design resource, such as a set of floor tiles, a piece of honeycomb, a sketch or photograph be translated into a quilt? There are actually many ways to do this, but for the quilts in this book I have used a quilt software program on my computer as well as my trusty pencil and paper.

Electric Quilt 5 and other quilt-related computer programs make it easy and fun to design your own quilts and to experiment with different colour combinations.

Computer Software

I have been using a software program called Electric Quilt 5, and although my skills with this program are still in their infancy, I am excited by its endless possibilities and find it an excellent resource. It just shows that it is never too late to learn a new skill. There are other quilt-related programs for you to try too, such as QuiltPro.

Friendship Twist (page 44), T Block (page 82) and Eastern Promise (page 98) were all designed using Electric Quilt 5 for the simple reason that they are square blocks, and working with these is well within the limited scope of my current skills. Although I coloured the designs on the computer, I used my own fabrics on a design wall to create the final result.

I used the Electric Quilt 5 software to help me design Oriental Kimonos (see page 82).

I used isometric paper to draft the design for Polka Dot Ragtime (see page 74) and the other Pine Bark quilts.

Paper and Pencil

For most of the quilts in this book I used graph paper and pencil to develop the designs. If the tessellation is made out of triangles, squares or rectangles then ¼in graph paper is ideal to work on because you can draw the blocks to size and it is easy to add the ¼in seam allowances. Any shape based on a diamond requires isometric graph paper (see below left). I used isometric paper to help me draft the designs of the Pine Bark quilts (see above and page 74).

I find it helpful to take a photograph of my inspiration so that I can have the image beside me when I start to draft the design. I begin by drawing a rough sketch of the tessellated shape on plain paper. This will not always fit into a square, and it is here that the graph paper comes into its own when I now translate the shape on to the grid. When I am happy with the basic block I find it useful to draft a number of the blocks on to a fresh sheet of graph paper and use these to experiment with different colour or tonal combinations. Often at this stage other secondary designs start to emerge that may suggest the use of an alternative set of fabrics from those originally intended or even result in a whole new quilt.

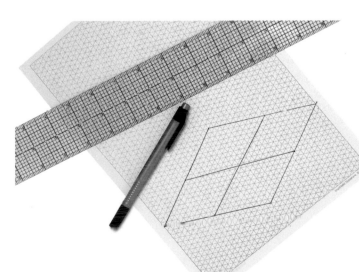

Isometric paper, as shown here, makes it possible to draw pattern pieces based on diamonds.

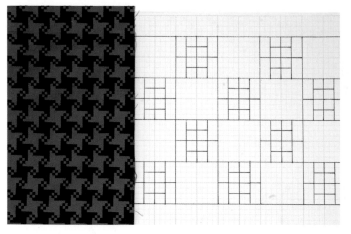

Place your reference material, or a photograph of it, beside you while you translate the design on to graph paper.

Now it is time to establish the correct size of the tessellated shape in order to calculate the final size of the quilt. I do this by drawing out the design in different sizes until I come up with a size that I feel works well.

Once I am satisfied with the block size I can add ¼in seam allowances to find the size of each piece. Most of my designs are based on simple geometrical shapes so it is an easy matter to cut the pieces, but sometimes it is necessary to draw up a template using template plastic or to buy one, as for the Pine Bark quilts (page 74). The diamond and triangle templates used in this book are available to purchase (see Useful Addresses, page 120). For information on making your own plastic templates see Sewing Basics, page 12.

Fabric Choices

The choice of fabric will have a dramatic effect on the look of the quilt. The most important factor is the fabric's colour value – whether it is dark, medium or light – because you need to make sure that there is sufficient contrast between the positive and negative shapes of the tessellation for the design to stand out.

As a general rule, consider your range of fabrics as an artist's palette. When making multicoloured tessellated quilts it is always better to cut a few more pieces than you need in a variety of fabrics that fall within the theme you have chosen. This will enable you to exchange fabrics on the design wall to ensure an effective result, and for me this is the most exciting part of the design process.

A simple way to ensure there is sufficient contrast between the positive and negative shapes of your design is to use one light or dark fabric for the negative spaces, as in Sweet Dreams (left and page 44) and Folk – Dancing (far right and page 84).

A design wall lets you see how the quilt will look before you have stitched the pieces together, making it possible to correct any design mistakes before you get too far down the line.

Design Wall

One of the most important steps in translating the tessellation into a quilt is the placement of the interlocking pieces. This needs to be done before you sew the fabrics together and you can only do this using a design wall (see Sewing Basics, page 10 and photograph above). The design wall enables you to stand back and see if the quilt would work better if elements are moved about or exchanged.

Cut out more pieces than you need so you can see how they work together and decide if anything jars and should be exchanged or if any fabric would work better in a different position.

Sewing Basics

Here are the instructions you'll need to help you prepare, cut and sew your fabrics together accurately. Even if you have already made quilts before it is worth reading this section because you may find my methods easier than those you have been using and you'll find some useful tips too.

Preparing your Fabric

Making a collection of fabrics to create quilts, whether they are inspired by tessellations or not, is a really enjoyable part of the process. But for tessellated quilts you need to buy a greater variety of co-ordinating fabrics than you might otherwise purchase and to buy when you see, because you might never find the same fabric again. The larger your fabric stash, the easier it is to choose the right colours for your quilt. Just think of it as your artist's palette.

The instructions in this book recommend cutting long strips, so it is better to buy long lengths rather than fat lengths. Some quilters wash their fabrics before sewing. I tend not to unless the quilt I am making is destined for a bed and will therefore have

to be washed at some point. If there is a particular fabric that I think might run or shrink, I wash it gently with a wool detergent, then rinse several times. If the colour continues to run, I will not use it.

Design Wall

When making tessellated quilts, a design wall is essential. It enables you to stand back and make decisions about the fabric placement before finally sewing the pieces together (see photograph on page 9).

To make a design wall in your sewing room, place some polystyrene or exhibition foam-core board (available from artists' suppliers), on the wall with an adhesive or use Velcro, as I do. Then use a heavy-duty stapler to attach a piece of cotton wadding/batting large enough to cover the area,

Design decision...

✔ Batik fabrics look wonderful and the process of making them generally involves repeated washing and rinsing so they are unlikely to shrink or run.

applying the staples around the edges. If you do not have an available wall, you can achieve the same effect but on a smaller scale by using a large piece of board and securing the batting over it. You can now just place the blocks or fabric pieces on the wadding/batting and they will stay there without pinning.

Rotary Cutting Equipment

For accurate cutting, good equipment is essential.

Rotary cutter Use one that is comfortable in your hand. Try out the various types at your local quilting shop or at a quilt show. A sharp blade brings greater accuracy to cutting.

Cutting table Your cutting table should be at a comfortable height for you to use standing up so that you can exert gentle pressure on the board with the cutter and not get backache in the process. House bricks or blocks of wood can be used to raise your table to the correct height.

Rulers It is easier and leads to fewer mistakes to cut using the correct width of ruler. I find the following sizes very useful: 2½, 3½, 4½ and 6½in. I also have a collection of squares in these sizes as well as much larger squares for squaring up the corners when the quilt is finished, prior to sewing on the binding. I use Creative Grids clear acrylic rulers because I find the non-slip spots on the back help to make cutting accurate (see Useful Addresses, page 120).

For making the quilts in this book I have also used some specialist rulers: the Diamond and Triangle templates and the Binding Mitre Tool for finishing off hexagonal corners of 120 degrees rather than the usual 90 degrees.

The larger your fabric stash, the easier it is to choose the right colours for your quilt. For Lavender Dream (left and page 70), I needed 30 different fabrics.

Cutting Fabric

The following instructions are for right-handed quilters. If you are left-handed you will need to reverse these instructions.

1 Press the fabric before cutting to eliminate any creases – these will distort your fabric pieces and result in inaccurate piecing.

2 Fold the fabric in half with the selvedge running from top to bottom and place it on the cutting board using a horizontal line near you as a straight edge guide.

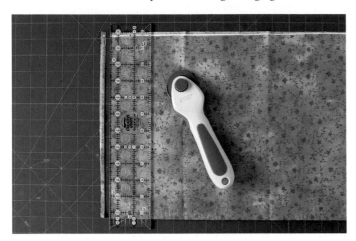

3 When cutting strips, place the ruler of the correct width vertically on the board to the right of the edge, and use the vertical lines on the board to match up top and bottom measurements. Always cut away from yourself and close the blade of the cutter as soon as you have cut the piece.

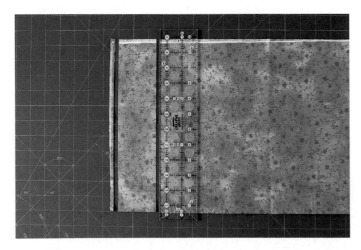

4 Holding the ruler down with your thumb and three fingers, place your little finger on the left edge of the ruler to stabilize it. Gently exert pressure on the cutter and cut away from yourself.

Making your own Templates

1 Draw up your design life size or, if using one of the templates in this book, scale it up to full size on a photocopier using the percentage enlargement provided. Tape the design to your work surface to hold it in place, then tape a sheet of template plastic over the design and use a fine permanent marker and ruler to trace the design precisely on top.

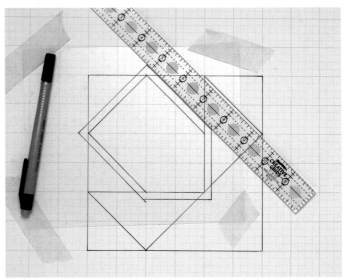

2 Cut out the template with paper scissors or an old rotary cutting blade. Place a coloured dot on the upper side of the template to make sure you cut out the fabric correctly and label the piece with a name, letter or number to avoid any confusion.

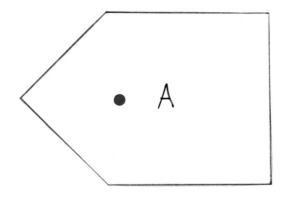

Don't forget to...

✔ Use the thickest template plastic you can buy when making your own templates. For strength, make several templates of the same piece and glue them together, leaving them overnight to set. Then label your template and it's ready to use.

Sewing Machine

There are many makes and models of sewing machine ranging from simple basic designs to elaborate electronic, computerized versions. The main functions needed to make the quilts in this book are straight sewing, a good satin stitch with variable width and the ability to do free-motion quilting with the feed dogs down or covered. The Husqvarna Viking SE that I use also has a scissors function, a fix stitch for securing the stitching and a needle down function, all of which are extremely useful when piecing and quilting. Good lighting on the needle is essential.

A reliable sewing machine is invaluable to the quilter.

Feet Required

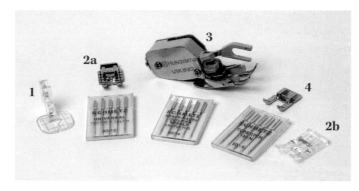

A selection of useful sewing machine needles and feet – their optimum uses are described below.

1 **Darning foot** When free-motion quilting, as when stippling, it is essential to use the correct foot for your machine. Some darning feet are open toed, others are made of a see-through plastic, but the most important feature is to be able to lower the feed dogs (or cover them up) so that you can manoeuvre the quilt sandwich freely as you quilt.
2 **(a and b) ¼in foot** The ability to sew a precise ¼in seam is essential for accuracy in piecing. Many machines now have

their own brand of ¼in foot. For those that do not, there are ¼in feet available to convert them. For details, ask your local dealer or a quilt shop that sells sewing machines.
3 **Walking foot** (sometimes called the quilting foot) This is a large foot with little feet beneath it that literally walk the quilt sandwich through the machine. This prevents puckers and tucks in the backing fabric. There are also open-toed walking feet available, which give a better view as you stitch. Ask your dealer for details.
4 **Open-toed foot** It is easier and more accurate to sew a satin stitch if the foot used is open toed as this gives an instant view of the stitch.

Machine Needles

A really sharp needle is essential for good stitching and the smooth running of your sewing machine. Change the needle frequently, particularly when sewing on batik and also when quilting. I recommend the following sizes:
• Size 70 for sewing on 100 per cent cotton batik, which has a high weave count.
• Size 80 for sewing and piecing on regular 100 per cent cotton.
• Quilting sizes 75–90 for quilting.
• Embroidery sizes 75–90 for satin stitch.

Piecing

To join pieces accurately, pin them at both ends and in the centre so any easing can take place in between. Always use a ¼in seam allowance. Use matching thread where possible, if not a dark beige or mid-grey should work with most fabrics.

Careful cutting and pinning helps to ensure successful piecing. This detail is from Pioneer Patches (see page 46).

Pressing

For accurate piecing it helps to press as you go. You are not ironing, but simply pressing. I use steam to get rid of creases and folds, otherwise a hot iron should be used to press seams to one side or open as you wish. A good iron and board at the right height, conveniently placed close to the sewing machine, helps enormously while piecing. I press my work as I go to make sure that I have achieved perfect points and matching seams. It is far easier to rectify this at the piecing stage rather than later when the quilt top is completed.

Fusing

Some quilts require fusing as a technique for adding fabric. Use a fusible web such as Bondaweb, Wonder Under or Steam a Seam, remembering that whichever side you trace on to, the image will turn out in reverse. Practise with one piece first to experiment. Use a warm to hot iron and follow the instructions here.

1   Trace the image on to fusible web and number it or give it a letter to avoid confusion later on.
2   Cut out the piece with a rough ¼in allowance all the way round.
3   Press the fusible web to the wrong side of the fabric, making sure that the edges do not go over the fabric and on to the ironing board.
4   Cut out the shape, peel off the backing paper and press on to the fabric in the required position using a warm to hot iron.
5   Secure the edges by working satin stitch around them, half on the fused piece and half on the background fabric.

When fusing fabrics...

✔ If fusible web gets on to your ironing board it leaves a sticky residue that attracts dirt and can stick to your clothes. To protect your ironing board either cover it with an old piece of fabric or a tea towel or buy a special fusible web pressing sheet to protect the surface. Ask at your local quilt shop for details.

Mitred Corners

When adding borders, a mitred corner gives a professional finish as you can see on Sunrise, Sunset (page 93) for example. Follow the instructions here to mitre the border on your quilt. To mitre binding, as on Cat's Cradle (page 52), you can use a binding mitre tool (see page 60).

1   Measure the width of the quilt.
2   Cut strips of border fabric to the width of the quilt plus twice the width of the border plus 3in.
3   Fold the border strip in half and mark the fold with a pin.

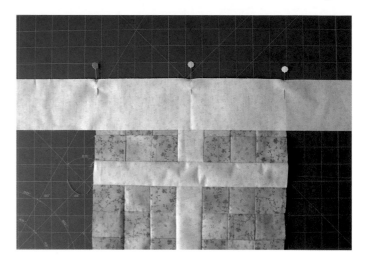

4   Measure half the quilt width in each direction from the pin and add another pin. These pins mark where the edges of the quilt will be. Pin the border in place.
5   Stitch the seam, starting and finishing ¼in inside each outer pin.

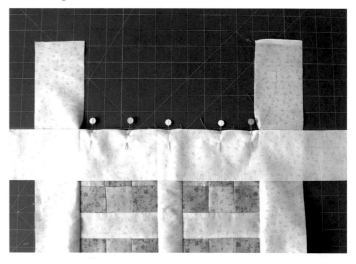

6   Add all the borders using this method.
7   Press the seam allowances towards the border strips.

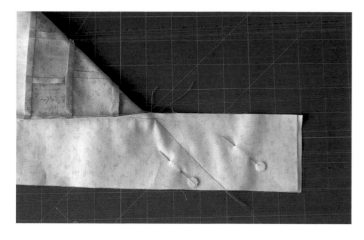

8 Lay adjacent borders over each other and pin. Draw a line at 45 degrees from the end of the border seam. Sew along that line from the corner to the edge.

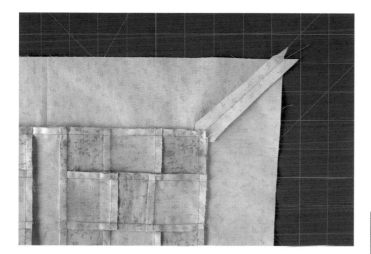

9 Trim away the waste then press the seam open.

10 Repeat at the remaining three corners and you will achieve perfect mitres.

Marking the Quilt Design

You can mark the quilt design before or after assembling the quilt sandwich. If you are free-motion machining you have no need to do this, and if you have decided to use a simple grid design you can mark the lines when the quilt sandwich is made. However, for fairly complex repeat patterns, such as leaves or feathers, you will find it easiest to mark the design before the quilt sandwich has been prepared. When machine quilting try to use continuous designs to prevent too many stops and starts.

There are many different quilting design sources available, from stencils to books of continuous patterns. You may have to enlarge or reduce them and make your own stencils by tracing through template plastic. You may even wish to incorporate a design inspired by the fabric or the name of the block or design you used to piece the quilt.

Choose the marker carefully, making sure that you can remove the marks by trying it out on spare pieces of fabric which you have used in the quilt. There are many different types of quilt marking pen and pencil available. I prefer to use chalk pencils, as I know I can remove the marks with an old toothbrush without wetting the quilt.

Mitred borders give a professional touch, as here, on Sunrise, Sunset (see page 93).

Another method of applying the quilting design is to use greaseproof paper. First trace the design on to ordinary paper to make sure you have the exact size. Now cut greaseproof paper the length of the stencil and fold it into as many folds as it will take. Press firmly. Pin the stencil on to the greaseproof paper and machine around the design using an old needle with no thread and using a small stitch length. You can now cut the folds in the paper and pin the designs to your quilt top. Machine along the lines. It will be easy to remove the greaseproof paper because you have already machined along the lines.

If the stitching design is fairly ornate, as on Beverley Mosaics (see page 53), it is easiest to mark it on the fabric before assembling the quilt sandwich.

Stitching in the Ditch

I find that stitching along all the seams helps to stabilize the quilt sandwich before I stitch my chosen quilting design. This is known as stitching in the ditch.

Making the Quilt Sandwich

This stage is crucial to the finished look of your quilt. Care taken now will give you a quilt to be proud of.

1 Press the quilt top and measure the width and the length.
2 Add at least 2–3in to this measurement and cut the backing and batting to that size. You may have to piece the backing. If so, take care to avoid a centre seam.
3 Fold the backing in half and place a pin to mark the halfway point on each end. Lay out the backing with the wrong side facing up and with the halfway-point marking pins showing. If using a table, secure the backing to it with masking tape at several points along the edges, smoothing it out until it is flat. If using the floor, pin along the edges, making sure it is flat.
4 Fold the batting in half and place a pin to mark the halfway point on each end. Lay the batting on top of the backing, matching the pins. Smooth out the batting.
5 Fold the quilt top in half and place pins to mark the halfway point on each end. Lay it over the batting, matching the halfway pins. Smooth it out.
6 You are now ready to use your preferred method of fixing the quilt sandwich together. If you are hand quilting, tack (baste) the layers together in a grid about 4in apart, using a contrasting thread. If you are machine quilting you can place 1in safety pins at frequent intervals across the quilt. (No larger, or you risk putting holes in the quilt.) If you are using a quilt tack gun, place a grid underneath and fire the tacks at frequent intervals. There are also quilt-basting sprays available, and you will have to apply the spray to each layer as you assemble the quilt sandwich.

Squaring Up the Corners

In order to ensure that your finished quilt will hang straight when it is completed you need to square up the corners. A large square ruler is far better than using a long ruler for this.

1 Place a large square ruler over the corner and square it up to just a little under ¼in beyond the outer edge.
2 Measure from the outer edge to the first border, making sure this measurement is the same on both edges. In this example (page 17, top left) the edge is 2¾in away from the border on both sides. Trim away any excess fabric.
3 Continue to square up the remaining three corners and complete the edges with a long ruler using the same measurement from the edge to the first border.

Stitching in the ditch (along the seam lines) helps to hold the quilt sandwich in place. The stitching will be barely visible if worked in invisible/monofilament thread.

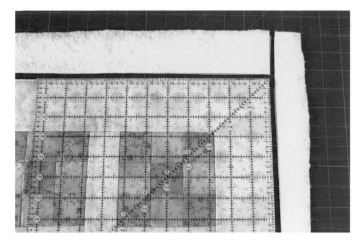

Use a large square ruler to help you square up the corners.

Attaching a Hanging Sleeve

If your quilt is to be hung on the wall a hanging sleeve will help to ensure that it hangs straight. It also spreads the hanging strain equally across the width.

1 Measure the width of the quilt and cut a 5½in strip just short of your measurement.
2 Press in the two outer short edges with a double fold to make hems. Make a single fold along one long edge to make another hem.
3 From the wrong side, stitch the hems in place.

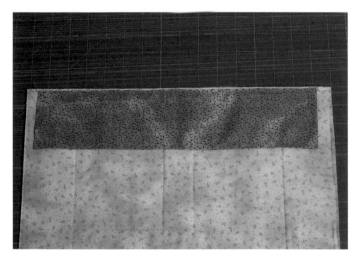

4 Place the sleeve centrally on the top back edge of the prepared quilt a little less than ¼in from the top.
5 Attach the sleeve with a tacking (basting) stitch ¼in from the edge of the quilt. This edge will be covered by the binding at the next stage.

Continuous Binding Strips

Usually you will need to join strips together to make a piece long enough to bind the quilt edges. Use diagonal seams, as explained here, which are less noticeable and also less bulky than sewing straight seams.

1 Cut sufficient strips for the required length.
2 Place two strips right sides together, overlapping at one end, one horizontally and the other vertically.

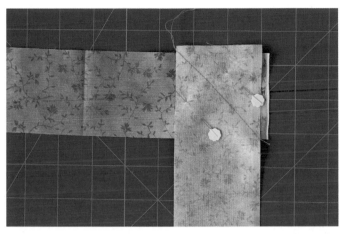

3 Use a fabric marker to draw a line at 45 degrees. Sew along the line.

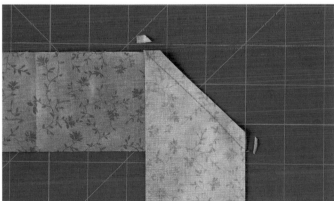

4 Now cut away the waste.

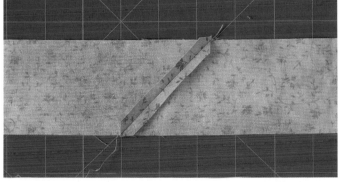

5 Press the seam open.

Binding the Edges

All the quilts in this book are finished with binding. It frames the quilt and gives a neat finish.

1 Cut strips 2½in wide and join them in a continuous strip as explained on page 17. Make the strip at least 3in longer than the quilt perimeter.

2 Press in half lengthways.

3 Press one end of the binding diagonally and trim away, leaving a generous ¼in.

4 Place the raw edge of the binding a scant ¼in in from the raw edge of the quilt, starting about halfway along one side. Check that the seam from joining the continuous strip does not end up at the corner.

5 Using a ¼in seam allowance, start sewing about 3in from the diagonal fold on the binding (see step 3) and stop ¼in from the corner. Sew diagonally into the corner. (This is a useful tip I picked up from Libby Lehmann.)

6 Fold the binding up.

7 Fold down the binding parallel with the edge and sew the next side, starting from the top of the quilt and keeping the ¼in seam allowance.

8 Continue until all the corners have been sewn.

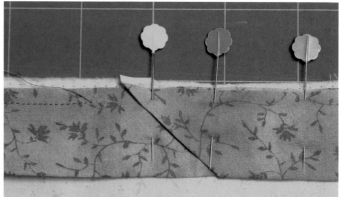

9 When you come towards your starting point, cut the binding to just more than the diagonal fold at the starting point and tuck the rest of the binding into the fold. Pin it firmly into place and sew down.

10 From the front of the quilt, press the binding away from the edge, using a medium-hot iron. Take care if you have used a polyester thread as this will melt.

11 Cut ¼in wide strips of Bondaweb, Wonder Under or Steam a Seam and press them on to the seam allowance on the back of the quilt, as shown above.

12 Peel off the paper and press the binding firmly down to the back of the quilt, taking care to mitre all the corners neatly, as shown.

13 Sew the two binding ends firmly into the diagonal seam.

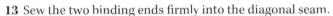

14 Hem the binding into place and you will have a perfect binding with mitred corners.

15 Now you can sew the hanging sleeve in place by making a slight gusset so that a hanging rod or pole will be taken up in it and not show at the front of the quilt.

Adding a Label

In years to come, a label on the back of the quilt containing its title, your name, the date and the town you live in will be an excellent reference. It will be particularly interesting for future generations. If the quilt is to be a gift, the label will be a permanent reminder of your friendship.

I made this label to go on the back of Tea Time (see page 83), printing on to cotton fabric that had been specially treated for the process.

19

Colour Confidence

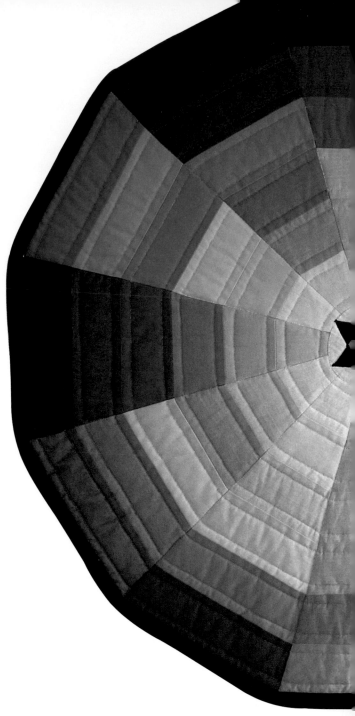

If you want to create your own colour combination for a tessellated quilt and don't know where to begin, here are some tips to get you started. Don't just walk into your local quilting shop and expect to pluck a 'game plan' out of the air. The array of different colours, styles and patterns is simply too vast and unless you have an idea of what you want before you go in, you can easily become confused.

Choosing a Colour Combination

• If your quilt is going to hang in a particular room, let the colours of the room or the occupant's favourite motifs lead the way. Cat's Cradle (see page 52), for example, was designed specifically to fit my grandson's bedroom.
• Look at the quilts in this book and think about using the colours in one quilt with another design. Notice how different the quilts in each chapter are, despite being worked in the

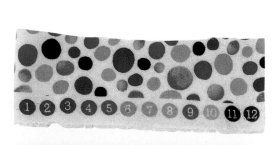

If you find it difficult to match colours to a focus fabric, a simple idea is to look at the selvedge. Here you'll see small samples of each colour used in the printing process; use this to help you find your matching fabrics.

same basic pattern, because of the colour and tonal changes. Look closely to decide which combinations you are drawn to.

• Look at fabrics in houses, shops or showrooms that you particularly like and take note of the colours used in them. If at all possible, keep a sample or take a photograph to help you remember.

• Look at Nature's palette. If you see a flower or view that takes your fancy, then pay close attention to its colours and tones. Remember that anything in Nature may inspire you, from a sunset (see Sunset at Sisters, page 48), to an aquarium or even something as small as a beetle.

• Start with a focus fabric. If you already have a fabric that you want to use or see one in a quilt shop, use this for your focus and build your design around it. This is where the artist's colour wheel comes in handy (see left). Colours next to each other on the wheel create a restful harmony, while opposites, which are called complementary colours, make each other 'sing' when placed together.

Don't forget to...

✔ Always take a compact camera with you, and whenever you see anything that you really like, just snap away. Digital cameras are great for this purpose because you can build up files of similar colours or themes on your computer and you can enlarge them to bring out colours you never realized were there. You can also view your images in black and white, helping you see the values more clearly.

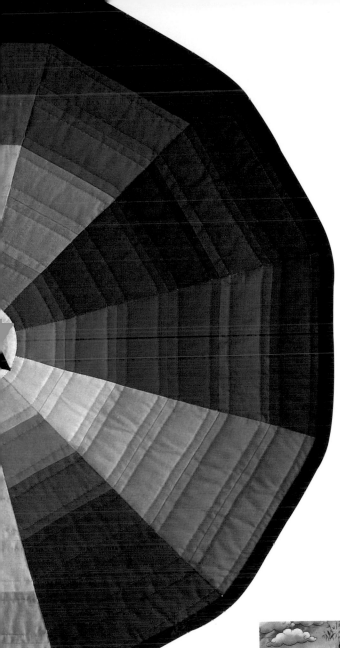

The colour wheel is useful for anyone working with colour. Use adjacent primaries, such as red and yellow, with some of the shades of orange and pink in between for a pleasant harmony. Use opposites for a dramatic and lively result.

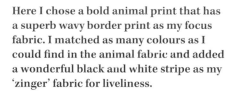

Here I chose a bold animal print that has a superb wavy border print as my focus fabric. I matched as many colours as I could find in the animal fabric and added a wonderful black and white stripe as my 'zinger' fabric for liveliness.

Using Tones or Values

Simply put, a colour's tone or value refers to how light or dark it is. When we start quilting we usually play safe and use a lot of medium valued fabrics. Later we learn to add lighter values and finally we choose the dark values that really bring out the contrast in the design.

A good tonal range is especially important in tessellated designs. This is because the design is made up of a repeated positive and negative pattern and if the tones of each are the same then the pattern will be lost. This is easier to understand if you look at the design in black and white as in Memories of Siena (see right and page 91).

When looking at your inspirational image, be it a fabric or flower, consider not just its colours but also its values. You may be surprised how varied these are even on something as mellow as a tulip (see below). Look, too, at the range of values

in my quilts to help you make the right choices. The three Churn Dash blocks shown here were all inspired by colour combinations I saw in life. Notice how varied the values are in each one. Also notice how the placement of the values draws attention to different elements in each sample.

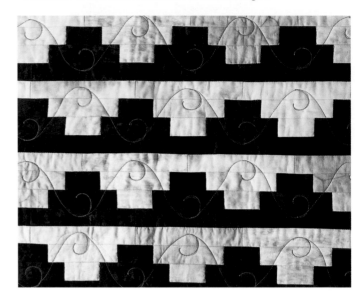

In Memories of Siena (above and page 91) you can clearly see the importance of tone for a tessellated design.

This tulip (below) utilizes a wonderful range from cream and pale pink to orange and red. Nature has complemented the flower with a range of greens from lime to dark green, and I have used these colours on the Churn Dash block, left.

Manmade objects can also inspire. The boat above, photographed in Cornwall, UK, inspired the fabric selection that I used for the Churn Dash block shown left.

Holidays can be a good time to find inspiration because we have the time and inclination to look around us and usually have our cameras to hand. The Guatemalan hammocks (below) inspired another colour combination (right).

23

Quilt Projects

There are nine totally different quilt designs in this section, all using tessellated patterns. Each basic pattern is interpreted in several different ways to enable you to see how even simple changes, such as altering the size of a block or changing the fabrics and border design can have a dramatic effect. I also hope that it will inspire you to make other changes and take over the design process yourself. I have certainly found it an endlessly fascinating subject and hope you will too.

Magical Maze

This design is well known in quilting and I was intrigued recently to find the pattern, which is reminiscent of dog-tooth check, on a contemporary silk tie worn by a young friend. It then turned up as the motif on a piece of dressmaking crêpe fabric from the early 1900s that I inherited from my mother-in-law, who was a great collector of fabric. While making the quilts for this chapter, I was excited to find the same pattern on a jacket worn by a neighbour. My version of this design is called Magical Maze and is extremely simple. Once the technique has been learned for putting the pieces together, the sky is the limit. The more different fabrics you use, the more fun you can have, and the best part is that you need very little of each one, which makes it an ideal design for scrap quilts.

Featured on the following pages are my seasonal designs, and further examples of how the pattern can be used. Instructions for making Summer are on pages 30–32.

SUMMER 28½ x 34in

Summer

I made four small wall hangings to celebrate the seasons and these can be changed around according to the time of year. The theme of summer made me think of tropical vegetation and I found a luscious print that inspired me. From the hectic colours of the large floral print, I chose hot reds, pinks, oranges, and a couple of pastels as a counterbalance. I found a superb lush green for the border and used my floral fabric as a binding to bring it all together and frame the quilt nicely.

Dog-tooth check on crêpe fabric, one of the original inspirations for Magical Maze.

The Changing Seasons

Spring (right) was inspired by some brightly coloured pansies in our garden and when I found the border fabric, I knew that it was exactly right for this quilt. For the inner crosses, I picked out shades of green, yellow and mauve to match the border fabric. A dark purple binding makes an excellent frame for this quilt. The Autumn quilt (below left) was inspired by a collection of leaves on a Virginia creeper that grew on the outside of our house. That particular autumn we had beautiful weather and the leaves turned amazing colours. I picked several leaves and rushed to my fabric stash to match them up. The surrounding purple-brown batik warns of the dark days approaching. For Winter (below right) I wanted to give the impression of cold, icy weather and had fun finding fabrics to match that theme. The variations of greys and whites give a shivery effect and surrounding them with black batik achieved my goal of creating harmony. A contemporary black-and-white stripe cut on the bias for the binding made a good framing statement.

SPRING 26½ x 32½in

AUTUMN 21½ x 33½in

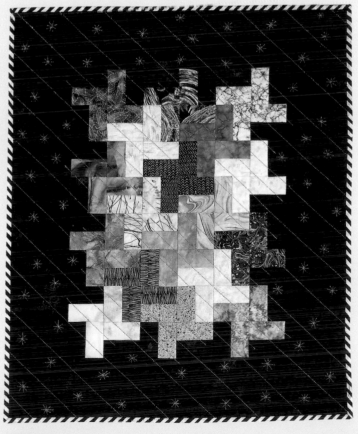

WINTER 28¼ x 34½in

Persian Carpet

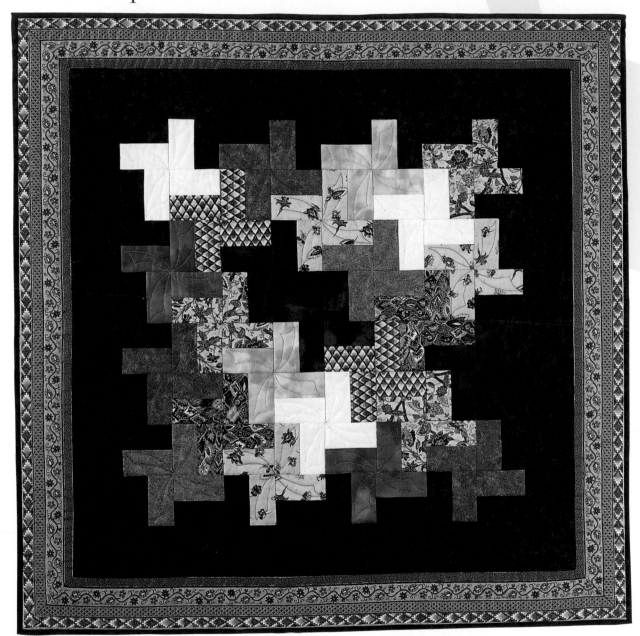

PERSIAN CARPET by Sally Ablett 36 x 36in

Sally chose an interesting range of fabric from Makower for this quilt and used coordinating plain fabrics to enhance the effect. The dark purple border seems to push the decorative centre of the quilt forward and provides 'breathing space' between this section and the pretty decorative border. Free-motion quilting of a leaf pattern in the crosses echoed by flowers and leaves in the purple background is set off by straight-line quilting in the border.

Mitred corners make the most of the pretty border fabric.

Magic Carpet

MAGIC CARPET 47½ x 47½in

In this larger version of the Magical Maze design I used a combination of several colours based on my focus fabric, which is the light floral fabric in the centre. I find that picking out all the colours from a focus fabric helps to harmonize a quilt and makes it easy on the eye. I chose shades of green, purple, yellow and pink and then a black background to contrast with the inner fabrics. This time, I added a wider border for emphasis and satin stitched a double row of rayon variegated thread to make an inner frame. For a quilting design, I made a plastic template of a reduced version of the crosses. Then, using metallic thread, I outlined them as a border pattern and added free-motion crosses to the centre of each. The binding was made by joining all the scraps of yellow fabrics left over from the central crosses.

Metallic thread provides an added dimension.

29

Quilt Size: 28½ x 34in

MATERIALS

Fabric
100% cotton fabrics 44in wide:
• ⅛ yard each of 24 different contrasting fabrics
• ¾ yard medium/dark green for background
• ½ yard floral fabric with a variety of large flowers for appliqué and binding

Batting
48 x 36in

Backing
1¼ yards of your choice

Rulers
2½ x 12½in
18½ x 6½in

Extras
Fusible web (Bondaweb or Wonder Under)

Please note…

✔ Diagrams show the fabric pieces without seam allowances for clarity.

Summer

CUTTING
Measurements include ¼in seam allowances.

Contrasting fabrics
Although you will only use 18 of these colours in the quilt, it is useful to have more so that you can substitute colours at the design stage.
From each of the 24 fabrics:
• 1 strip (2 x 15in). Cut into 4 rectangles (2 x 3½in)

Medium/dark green for background
• 2 strips (2 x 44in). Cut into 24 rectangles (2 x 3½in)
• 4 strips 5½in
  Cut into 2 strips 24½in long
  Cut into 2 strips 28½in long

Floral for appliqué and binding
• 3 strips 2½in wide

Don't forget to…

✔ Use a design wall to help in the placement of the blocks. You can then stand back and judge the design before sewing, as you may wish to change some of the blocks around. (See Sewing Basics, page 10.)
✔ Press the fabric before cutting. I use a fabric stabilizer or starch on the reverse side of the fabric. This makes for more accurate cutting, especially on long strips.

METHOD
Designing the Interior of the Quilt
1 Lay out the 24 piles of 4 strips (2 x 3½in) in a row next to your design wall.
2 Starting in the top left-hand corner, arrange the first four strips of one colour (**Fig 1a**).

3 Take a contrasting colour and arrange the next 4 strips, as shown (**Fig 1b**). During the design process, as you arrange the strips on the design wall, you will have to overlap the second colour where the two horizontal or vertical rectangles are placed next to each other, to make them fit into the space available. This is only temporary – once they are sewn with the ¼in seam allowance, they will fit perfectly.
4 Continue to build up your design (**Fig 1c**).
5 Complete the design as in the photograph, left, using 18 different colours. When you are happy with the arrangement, place the 24 medium/dark green background rectangles (2 x 3½in) in the gaps around the edges (**Fig 1d**).

Fig 1a

Fig 1b

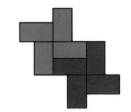

Fig 1c

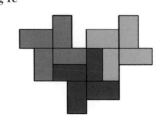

Fig 1d

Fig 2a

Fig 2b

Fig 2c

Assembling the Quilt

1 Take the first pair of rectangles in the top left-hand corner and sew them together (**Fig 2a**). Press the seam towards the dark fabric.

2 Sew the top row of rectangles together as described above and then join to make a row (**Fig 2b**).

3 Sew the rest of the rectangles together row by row and then join the rows together and press (**Fig 2c**). Press the horizontal seams open. This makes the quilt lie flatter for quilting later on.

Borders

1 Measure from the top to the bottom of the quilt through the centre. This should be 24½in.

2 Sew 2 border strips (5½ x 24½in) to each side of the quilt and press towards the border.

3 Measure from side to side across the centre. This should be 28½in.

4 Sew the 2 remaining border strips (5½ x 28½in) to each side of the quilt and press towards the border (**Fig 3**).

Floral Appliqué

There are several methods for appliqué. Here is the one used for this quilt.

1 Carefully choose the flowers you wish to appliqué around the borders from the remaining floral fabric.

2 Turn the fabric over so that the reverse side is uppermost.

Fig 3

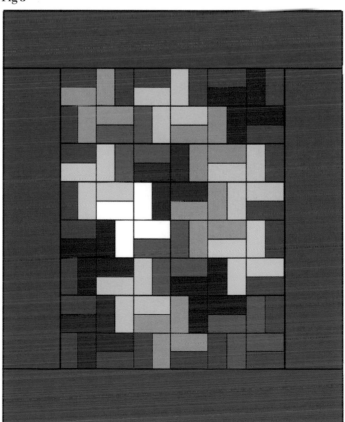

3 Cut pieces of fusible web slightly larger than the outline of the flowers.

4 Cut away the inside of the fusible web to within ¼–½in from the edge of the flowers.

5 Press on to the back of the flowers.

6 Cut out around the outline of each flower and peel off the backing paper.

7 Place the flowers carefully on to the quilt and press.

8 Using a narrow-width satin stitch, neatly machine around the outside of the flowers.

QUILTING & FINISHING
Backing

1 Cut the backing fabric to fit the quilt, allowing 2in extra all the way round. Press open any seams.

2 Cut the batting to the same size.

Quilting

1 Make the quilt sandwich of top, batting and backing and secure with safety pins, quilt tacks or basting spray if machine quilting, or by tacking if hand sewing. Refer to Sewing Basics, page 16.

2 Quilt as desired. This quilt was quilted in the ditch along most of the seams to stabilize the blocks. A meandering design with matching threads was free-motion quilted on all the blocks and the border has a free-motion quilted floral meandering design. I outlined the petals on the appliquéd flowers with free-motion quilting using matching threads.

Binding and Finishing

1 Measure the perimeter of the quilt and join the 2½in floral strips in a continuous strip to match your measurement, plus 3in.

2 Fold in half along the length and press flat.

3 Refer to Sewing Basics, pages 17–19, for details on how to attach the binding, label and hanging sleeve.

As an extra touch, I appliquéd some of the larger flowers around the border. The interior crosses were free-motion quilted with matching threads in a meandering design, while the border was free-motion quilted with flowers.

Free-motion quilting on the blocks.

Creative Options

For extra creativity, you can experiment, as I have, with adding appliqué, embellishing with various threads and different kinds of quilting.

SPRING When it came to the quilting, I satin stitched the outer edges of the crosses with purple thread to emphasize the colours and then free-motion quilted leaves in each cross with thread matching all the different colours. In the border I outlined the pansies with monofilament/invisible thread.

AUTUMN I used the reverse appliqué method to give the impression of falling autumnal leaves in the border and outlined them in green buttonhole stitch. Wanting to continue with a theme of autumnal windy days, I chose bronze and gold metallic thread to stitch swirling patterns across the whole quilt.

WINTER With the monochromatic colours of black, grey and white the quilting needed to reflect the stark simplicity of the design. Diagonal lines drawn in chalk and then quilted in silver metallic thread in a large stitch and the addition of free-motion silvery snowflakes in the border completed the wintry look.

Porter's Puzzle

An American friend sent me a small piece of black and purple fabric that was a variation of the dog-tooth check pattern. I immediately saw possibilities for translating it into a quilt, since the design was an outstanding example of a tessellation with identical positive and negative interlocking shapes. To work out the piecing, I drafted the pattern on ¼in graph paper and found it quite simple to make using the strip piecing method.

I have looked in many books on quilt blocks and have found no reference to this one, so I have named this original design Porter's Puzzle. The design lends itself to many alternative settings, a few of which are shown on the following pages. Instructions for making Memories of Japan and Californian Colour Waves are given on pages 39–43.

MEMORIES OF JAPAN 41 x 41in

Memories of Japan

This quilt uses the block in a basic setting with straight borders. It requires only two fabrics for the interior section: the main floral fabric, which has a Japanese style, and a dark green background fabric. The design does not touch the sashing and thus gives a feeling of floating within the interior of the quilt. The outer dark red border, with a bamboo motif, continues the Japanese theme and picks up the red in the focus fabric, while the inner pale green sashing and binding has a Sashiko design.

The fabric that originally inspired the design of Porter's Puzzle.

CALIFORNIAN COLOUR WAVES 41½ x 41½in

Californian Colour Waves

This design is created using nine interestingly coloured hand-dyed fabrics for the focus blocks. These stand out against the contrasting black background, giving the design a spiralling effect. The pale but muted tones of the batik sashing are a foil to the off-centre swirling and richly coloured batik border fabric. The dark purple binding encloses the colours without detracting from the diverse coloured sections of the quilt. Setting the inner design at this unusual angle makes it appear completely different visually.

A single block of Californian Colour Waves, showing how it interlocks with the neighbouring blocks.

Cats for Hannah

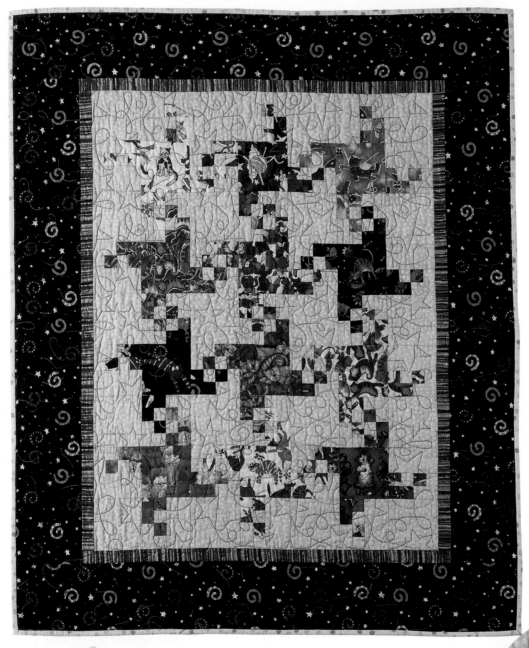

CATS FOR HANNAH 40 x 49½in
Quilted by Jenny Spencer

This quilt was made using the basic Porter's Puzzle block design, but each of the 12 contrast blocks is made up from a different cat fabric. It is an ideal pattern for children who love fantasy, fun and brightly coloured fabrics. When cutting the central squares it is important to ensure that the characters are centrally placed. The striped multicoloured sashing brings together all the colours used in the cat fabrics, while the black of the jazzy border enriches the bright yellow background in the inner part of the quilt. Bright yellow binding echoes the centre background to complete the look and draw the eye back into the centre.

The large black squares are 'fussy cut' with the cat motifs nicely centred.

Jazzy Illusions

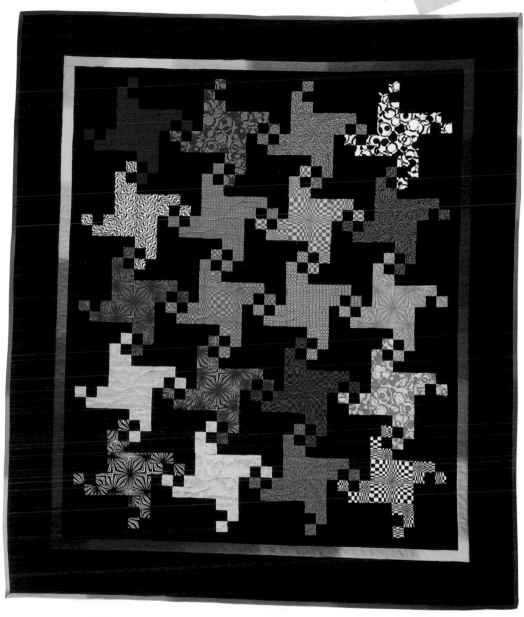

This wall hanging is a larger version of the Porter's Puzzle design, with 20 contrasting fabrics in black and white and primary colours on an Op Art theme. Here the placement of the different colours is important as they need to have a randomly spaced look with plenty of contrast between the light, medium and dark values. The black background provides an excellent foil to the bright colours and makes them stand out. The graded yellow to dark red sashing fabric emphasizes those colours within the quilt, while the graded green to purple binding pulls out the remaining colours. The dimensions of this quilt can easily be adjusted by increasing or decreasing the number of blocks.

JAZZY ILLUSIONS 53 x 46in
Quilted by Rosemary Archer

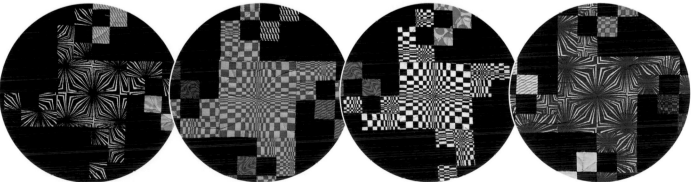

Careful selection of fabric details creates 'movement' in the blocks.

Up, Out and Into the Light

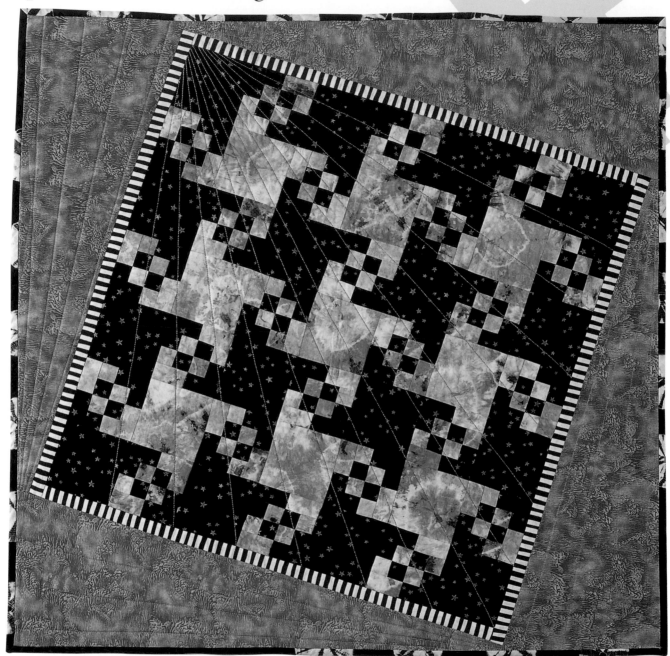

UP, OUT AND INTO THE LIGHT 39½ x 39½in

In this variation the pattern continues out to the sashing, giving a sense of going on into infinity. Since the pattern repeat is made in only two colours, it is quite easy to strip piece more units. The bold black and white striped sashing makes a strong visual statement and contains the interior pattern, emphasizing its off-set position within the quilt. A darker gold, slightly directional fabric in the border highlights the darker gold features of the inner gold squares. The long lines of gold metallic quilting in the interior and matching rich orange for the borders emphasizes the geometry of the design, while the binding of Japanese black and white Shibori fabric echoes the bold black-and-white stripe of the sashing.

Gold metallic machine quilting radiates from a corner of the inner quilt to add dynamism.

Quilt Size: 41½ x 41½in

Californian Colour Waves

MATERIALS

Fabric

A variety of 100% cotton fabrics 44in wide:
- ¾ yard black for background
- ¼ yard (fat) each of 9 different contrasting colours
- ¼ yard pale contrast for sashing
- ¾ yard medium for borders
- ¼ yard dark for binding

Batting

44in square

Backing

1¼ yards of your choice

Rulers

4½in square
2½ x 12½in
18½ x 6½in

CUTTING

Measurements include ¼in seam allowances.

Black for background

- 2 strips (4½in wide). Cut into 16 squares (4½in)
- 2 strips (2½in wide)
- 2 strips (2½in wide). Cut into 12 rectangles (2½in x 4½in)
- 4 strips (1½in wide)

9 contrast fabrics

From each cut:
1 square (4½in)
1 strip (2½ x 13in)
1 strip (1½ x 7in)

Pale contrast for sashing

4 strips (1½in wide)

Medium for borders

2 rectangles (12 x 30in)

Dark for binding

3 strips (2½in wide)

BLOCK ASSEMBLY

Finished block size 2 x 4in

1   Lay the 9 x 1½in contrast fabric

Don't forget to...

✔ Use a design wall to help in the placement of the blocks. You can then stand back and judge the design before sewing, as you may wish to change some of the blocks around. (See Sewing Basics, page 10.)
✔ Press the fabric before cutting. I use a fabric stabilizer or starch on the reverse side of the fabric. This makes for more accurate cutting, especially on long strips.

strips end to end along the black 1½in strip, right sides together, and stitch along the length (**Fig 1a**). Press the seam towards the black fabric strip.

2   Cut the strips apart into their separate colours. Then cut each colour strip in half and join the two halves together. Finally cut into 4 strips 1½in wide (**Fig 1b**).

3   Sew the 13 x 2½in contrast fabric strips to the 2½in black strip as in step 1 and press the seam towards the black fabric (**Fig 1c**).

4   Cut the strips apart into their separate colours. Then cut each

Fig 1a

Fig 1b

Fig 1c

colour section into 4 strips 1½in wide (**Fig 1d**).

5 Matching up the groups of 9 colours, sew the strips into 4 units of each colour (**Fig 1e**). *It is very important that you sew them together this way round* (otherwise they come out backwards and you cannot tessellate them).

Fig 1d

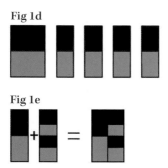

Fig 1e

Background and Coloured Squares (finished size 4in)

Take the 16 black 4½in squares and the 9 contrasting 4½in squares and place them on the design wall (see Sewing Basics page 10), as shown in **Fig 2**. They should fit together precisely and not overlap. This will make the quilt assembly much easier later on.

Fig 2

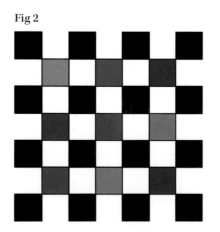

Assembling the Inner Quilt

1 Place the blocks in the gaps on the design wall, filling in the outer edges with the 12 black rectangles (4½in x 2½in). Make sure that the units are the right way round so that the blocks will tessellate – refer to **Fig 3**.

Fig 3

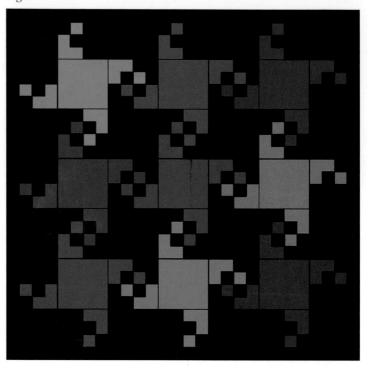

2 Now join the blocks and squares in rows and then join the rows. You will find it easier and more accurate when joining the rows to press one row in one direction and the next row in the opposite direction.

Sashing

1 Measure across the width of the quilt and cut 2 of the 1½in sashing strips to this length. (This quilt measured 28½in.)

2 Sew the strips to each side of the quilt and press seams towards the outside.

3 Measure across the length of the quilt and cut two more 1½in sashing strips to this length. Sew these to the remaining two sides and press seams to the outside. (This quilt measured 30½in.)

Off-set Border

1 Lay out the 2 rectangles (12 x 30in) of border fabric right sides up.

2 Cut into half along the diagonal (**Fig 4a** and **4b**).

3 Leaving 1½in at the square end, *beyond the edge of the quilt*, sew A to the top quilt edge.

4 Then sew on B, followed by C and D (**Fig 4c**).

5 Use a large square ruler to check that the corners are square.

Fig 4a

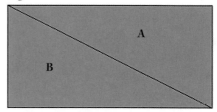

Fig 4b

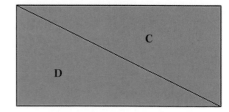

Porter's Puzzle

Quilting

1   Make the quilt sandwich of top, batting and backing and secure with safety pins, quilt tacks or basting spray if machine quilting, or by tacking if hand sewing. (See Sewing Basics, page 16.)

2   Quilt as desired. This quilt was quilted in the ditch with invisible/monofilament thread along most of the seams to stabilize the blocks, then free-motion quilted with matching thread in circles and rectangles on the coloured areas. The border was echo quilted on either side of a freehand drawn line using the width of the free-motion foot as a guide.

Binding and Finishing

1   Measure the perimeter of the quilt and join the 2½in dark binding strips in a continuous strip to match your measurement, plus 3in.

2   Fold in half along the length of the strip and press flat.

3   Refer to Sewing Basics, pages 17–19, for details on how to attach the binding, label and hanging sleeve.

Fig 4c

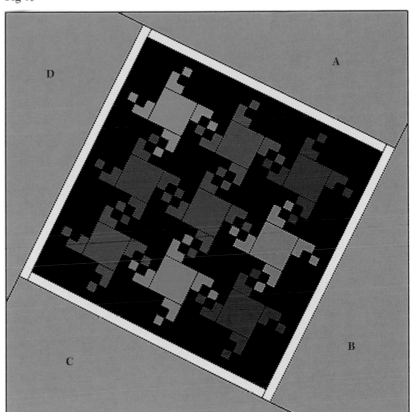

41

Quilt Size: 41 x 41in

MATERIALS

Fabric
100% cotton fabrics 44in wide:
• ¾ yard dark green for background
• 1 yard Japanese floral
• ½ yard mid green for sashing and binding
• ¾ yard dark red for borders

Batting
44in square

Backing
1½ yards of your choice

Rulers
4½in square
2½ x 12½in
18½ x 6½in

Don't forget to...

✔ Use a design wall to help in the placement of the blocks. You can then stand back and judge the design before sewing, as you may wish to change some of the blocks around. (See Sewing Basics, page 10.)
✔ Press the fabric before cutting. I use a fabric stabilizer or starch on the reverse side of the fabric. This makes for more accurate cutting, especially on long strips.

Memories of Japan

CUTTING
Measurements include ¼in seam allowances.

Dark green for background
• 2 strips (4½in wide). Cut into 16 squares (4½in)
• 2 strips (2½in wide)
• 2 strips (2½in wide). Cut into 12 rectangles (4½ x 2½in)
• 4 strips (1½in wide)

Japanese floral
• 9 squares (4½in). 'Fussy cut' with the flowers centred as follows: place the 4½in square ruler over the large flowers until you have the middle of a flower in the centre of the square, then cut around the square ruler (see the quilt photograph on page 34).
• 2 strips (2½in wide)
• 4 strips (1½in wide)

Mid green
• 4 strips (1½in wide) for sashing
• 4 strips (2½in wide) for binding

Dark red (for borders)
• 4 strips (4¼in wide)

BLOCK ASSEMBLY
Finished block size 4in square
1 Join one long 1½in dark green strip and one 1½in Japanese floral strip along the length, right sides together.
2 Press the seam towards the dark fabric.
3 Repeat with the remaining three pairs of dark and floral 1½in strips.
4 Join two strips together across the width so that you have: dark, light, dark, light. Press seams towards the dark fabric; repeat.
5 Cut each section into 1½in widths (**Fig 1a**). Make 36.

Design decision...

✔ You may wish to change around some of the colours at this stage as they look different when surrounded by the background colour.

---

6 Join one long 2½in dark green strip to a matching Japanese floral strip along the length with right sides together.
7 Press the seam towards the dark fabric.
8 Repeat with the remaining 2½in dark and floral strips. Press seams towards the dark fabric.
9 Cut each section into 1½in widths (**Fig 1b**). Make 36.
10 Sew the strips into units as shown in **Fig 1c**. Make 24 units. *It is very important that you sew them together this way round* (otherwise they come out backwards and you cannot tessellate them).
11 Join 2 units (**Fig 1d**) to make 12 blocks A.
12 Sew the remaining 12 units to the 12 dark green rectangles (2½ x 4½in) to make 12 blocks B (**Fig 1e**).

Fig 1a

Fig 1b

Fig 1c   **Fig 1d**

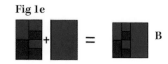

Fig 1e

Fig 2a

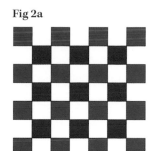

Fig 2b

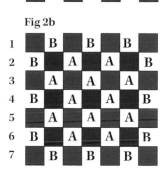

1		**B**	**B**		**B**	
2	**B**		**A**	**A**		**B**
3		**A**	**A**	**A**		
4	**B**		**A**	**A**		**B**
5		**A**	**A**	**A**		
6	**B**		**A**	**A**		**B**
7		**B**	**B**		**B**	

Assembling the Inner Quilt

1 Place the 16 dark green 4½in squares and the 9 floral 4½in squares on the design wall, as shown in **Fig 2a**. They should fit together precisely and not overlap. This will make the quilt assembly much easier later on.

2 Referring to **Figs 2b** and **3**, add blocks A and B (12 of each). Note that in rows 2, 4 and 6 the top of block A is set horizontally and in rows 3 and 5 the top of block A is set vertically. Similarly, note the different orientations of blocks B in each row – see **Fig 3** and the photograph on page 34. It is important to ensure that the units are the right way round so that the blocks tessellate correctly.

3 Now join the blocks in horizontal rows and then join the rows together. You will find it easier and more accurate when joining the rows to press one row in one direction and the next row in the opposite direction.

Sashing

1 Measure across the width of the quilt and cut two of the mid-green

Fig 3

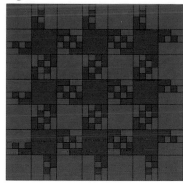

1½in strips to this length. (This quilt measured 28½in.)

2 Sew a strip to opposite sides of the quilt and press seams towards the outside (**Fig 4**).

3 Measure down the length of the quilt and cut two more mid-green 1½in strips to this length. (This quilt measured 30½in.) Sew these to the remaining sides; press seams.

Border

1 Measure across the width of the quilt and cut two of the dark red 4½in strips to this length. (This quilt measured 30½in.)

2 Sew the strips to the top and bottom of the quilt and press seams towards the outside.

3 Measure down the length of the quilt and cut two more dark red 4½in strips to this length. Sew these to the remaining sides and press the seams to the outside (**Fig 4**).

Fig 4

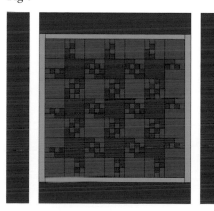

Backing

1 Cut the backing fabric to fit the quilt, plus a 2in overlap all the way round. Press open any seams.

2 Cut the batting to the same size.

Quilting

1 Make the quilt sandwich of top, batting and backing and secure with safety pins, quilt tacks or basting spray if machine quilting, or by tacking if hand sewing. (See Sewing Basics, page 16.)

2 Quilt as desired. This quilt was quilted in the ditch with invisible/ monofilament thread along most of the seams to stabilize the blocks before changing to matching thread and quilting free-motion flowers and leaves in the dark green areas. The Japanese floral fabric was free motion quilted with invisible/ monofilament thread outlining the leaves and petals. The border was free-motion quilted with red thread.

3 Large flowers from the remaining Japanese floral fabric were appliquéd on with a very small satin stitch around the border after the quilting was complete.

Binding and Finishing

1 Measure the perimeter of the quilt and join the 2½in mid-green strips in a continuous strip to match your measurement, plus 3in. (See Sewing Basics, page 17.)

2 Fold in half along the length of the strip and press flat.

3 Refer to Sewing Basics, pages 17–19 for details on how to attach the binding, label and hanging sleeve.

Please note...

✔ Diagrams show the fabric pieces without seam allowances for clarity.

Friendship Twist

The Friendship Star is a traditional design that is often chosen by members of quilting groups for quilts to welcome new members. In this version the arms of the star have a triangle that is added in a different colour to create a quarter-square triangle block. The stars then form a tessellation in strong diagonal lines in both directions, highlighting the background and the contrasting block fabrics.

It is rare that a tessellation can be formed from a square, but this is an exception, making it easy to explore variations using a software program such as Electric Quilt 5. Although I used this program, I still draw much of my inspiration from the actual fabrics. Notice how the use of diverse fabrics, the changes in the size of the blocks and the addition of different borders make each quilt unique.

Sweet Dreams

This candy-coloured quilt was largely inspired by a fabric collection by Darlene Zimmerman and has a 1940s look. I had a reasonable amount of the mid-blue floral, which I was able to use in the quarter-square triangle blocks and for the binding, but I had much less of the other colourful fabrics. After I had cut the 20 blocks my options for the sashing were limited, so I made narrow strips with eight of them and cut the yellow fabric into four small squares for the corners. I was very happy with the results because the sashing contributes to the look of a scrap quilt that I was aiming for. The cream border was wide enough for some special quilting. To relieve some of the plain colour, I featured smaller Friendship Stars in the corners. Instructions for making Sweet Dreams begin on page 49.

SWEET DREAMS 42½ x 50in
Quilted by Rosemary Archer

The small quarter-square triangle block frequently occurs in floor tiles either as border patterns or as an all-over design as here, in the Baptistery in Florence.

WATERMELON SURPRISE 41½ x 41½in

Quilted by Rosemary Archer

Watermelon Surprise

It is easy to see where the title of this quilt comes from: I used dark, medium and light values of red and green for a mouth-watering effect and arranged the fabrics to create a bold diagonal pattern. The bright lime green and deep, dark red of the quarter-square triangle blocks provide a perfect foil for the quieter colours of the star blocks. Note how they flip position as they run in diagonal rows from top right to bottom left and from top left to bottom right. A wide frame with contrasting corner blocks, each containing a star in a different fabric, emphasizes the square format of the design and draws the eye towards the colourful centre.

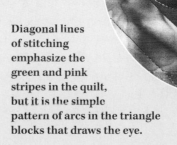

Diagonal lines of stitching emphasize the green and pink stripes in the quilt, but it is the simple pattern of arcs in the triangle blocks that draws the eye.

Pioneer Patches

PIONEER PATCHES 42 x 42in
Quilted by Rosemary Archer

As in Watermelon Surprise (page 45) straight lines of quilting are used to emphasize the diagonals. Hearts inside starbursts add a surprising but delightful new element.

A set of fat quarters in soft, vintage colours inspired this design. With just 16 blocks to play with, I decided to use the red and a pretty pink floral on cream for the dominant quarter-square triangle blocks. I needed contrast between the stars so I added some pale fabrics covered with tiny patterns to act as the lighter element. To help create the cosy look I associate with Pioneer quilts, I used two rows of sashing and made a decorative border by placing Flying Geese units alongside each other. A dark red binding completes the quilt and draws us back in to the dark red of the small squares.

Summer Meadow

SUMMER MEADOW 35 x 44in
Quilted by Rosemary Archer

For this design I pulled out a multitude of diverse fabrics and sat among them on the floor. Sitting there, the colourful effect made me feel as if I was surrounded by a field of summer flowers. It was surprisingly easy to come up with an attractive design using colours that really do not 'go' with each other provided that they are arranged in a random way. To contain my summer 'flowers' I added a border of pale but 'garden' green and made the little quarter-square blocks in a slightly paler green with dark green to continue the meadow theme. The dark green binding frames the quilt and echoes the dark green of the quarter-square triangles.

Swirling stitching at the centre of the main blocks shows that these are meadow stars or flowers.

Sunset at Sisters

SUNSET AT SISTERS 38 x 46in
Quilted by Rosemary Archer

I made this quilt to remind me of the happy times I spent teaching at the outdoor quilt show in Sisters, Oregon, run by Jean and Valori Wells, and the spectacular sunsets I saw there. The stars are made from just four fabrics; deep red, fiery orange, yellow and sage green. They act as a perfect foil for the tile-like black and cream quarter-square triangle blocks. While I was placing the pieces on my design wall I chose to emphasize the top and left-hand edge by filling in the spaces between the stars with the cream, which I then took out into the border. The stars at the bottom and right-hand edge stop at the vibrant border of yellow, gold and red, turning to deep red exactly as I had seen the sunset in Sisters.

The mitred border and lines of quilting stitches emphasize the diagonal progression of the design. Notice how the decorative stitches look like flaming hearts, emphasizing the passion and drama of the quilt.

Sweet Dreams

Quilt Size: 42½ x 50in

MATERIALS

Fabric
100% cotton fabrics 44in wide:
• ¼ yard of 10 contrasting fabrics
• ¾ yard mid-blue
• 1¾ yards cream

Batting
48 x 56in

Backing
2 yards of your choice

Rulers
2½ x 12½in

CUTTING
Measurements include ¼in seam allowances.

10 contrast fabrics
From each cut:
1 strip 2½ x 44in. Cut into 8 rectangles (2½ x 4½in)

4 of your 10 contrast fabrics
From each cut:
• 1 strip 1½ x 20in for sashing
• 4 squares 2½in for the corner stars
• 1 strip 1½ x 8in. Cut into 4 squares (1½in) for the corner stars

4 more of the contrast fabrics
From each cut:
1 strip 1½ x 16½in for sashing

1 of the remaining contrast fabrics (yellow)
4 squares (1½in) for the sashing

Cream fabric
• 9 strips (2½ x 44in). Cut into 80 rectangles (2½ x 4½in)
• 5 strips (2½ x 44in). Cut into 80 squares (2½in)
• 4 strips (4½in wide) for the border
• 1 strip (1½ x 44in). Cut into 12 strips (1½ x 3½in) for the corner stars

Mid-blue
5 strips (2½ x 44in). Cut into 80 squares (2½in)
4 strips (2½ x 44in) for the binding

Don't forget to...

✔ Use a design wall to help in the placement of the blocks. You can then stand back and judge the design before sewing, as you may wish to change some of the blocks around.

BLOCK ASSEMBLY
BLOCK 1
Finished block size 8in square

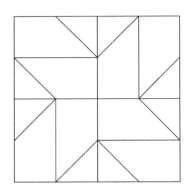

1   With right sides facing, place a 2½in mid-blue square exactly over the corner of a 2½ x 4½in cream rectangle and sew along the diagonal (**Fig 1a**).
2   Cut away the corner ¼in beyond the sewing line (**Fig 1b**).

Fig 1a   Fig 1b

3   Press the blue fabric away from the corner (**Fig 1c**). Repeat with three more cream rectangles.
4   With right sides facing, place a 2½in cream square exactly over the corner of a 2½ x 4½in coloured rectangle and sew along the diagonal (**Fig 1d**).

Fig 1c   Fig 1d

5   Cut away the corner ¼in beyond the sewing line (**Fig 1e**).
6   Press the coloured fabric away from the corner (**Fig 1f**). Repeat with three more coloured rectangles.

Fig 1e   Fig 1f

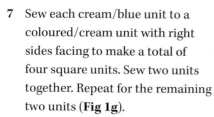

7 Sew each cream/blue unit to a coloured/cream unit with right sides facing to make a total of four square units. Sew two units together. Repeat for the remaining two units (**Fig 1g**).

8 Sew the two units together to make the block (**Fig 1h**). Repeat for the remaining 19 blocks to make two in each colour.

Fig 1g

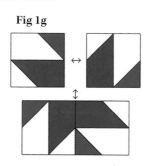

Fig 1h

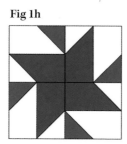

Assembling the Inner Quilt

1 Place the blocks on your design wall horizontally in five rows of four blocks. Sew four blocks together in a horizontal row (**Fig 2**).

2 Join the horizontal rows together to form the interior of the quilt.

Don't forget to...

✔ **Press the horizontal seams open. This makes the quilt lie flatter for quilting later on.**

Sashing

1 Arrange the strips of contrasting fabrics around the outside of the quilt. Sew two 20in strips together to make a long strip. Repeat with the remaining long strips. Sew these to each long side of the quilt.

2 Sew two 16½in strips together as before. Repeat with the remaining 16½in strips. Sew a 1½in (yellow) square to each end.
Sew these strips to the top and bottom of the quilt (**Fig 3**).

Fig 2

Fig 3

BORDER BLOCK

BLOCK 2
Finished block size 4in square

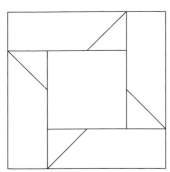

1 With right sides facing, place a 1½in contrasting square exactly over the corner of a 1½ x 3½in cream strip and sew along the diagonal (**Fig 4a**).

2 Cut away the corner ¼in beyond the seam line (**Fig 4b**).

3 Press the corner flat (**Fig 4c**). Make three more identical strips.

Fig 4a   Fig 4b   Fig 4c

4 Sew one strip across the top of a matching 2½in square, starting ¼in from the inner edge. Sew the remaining three strips to the square and to the end of the adjacent strip in the order shown (**Fig 4d**).

5 Complete the last seam and press the block flat (**Fig 4e**).

6 Make three more corner blocks with the remaining contrast fabrics.

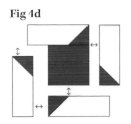
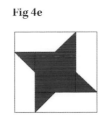

Fig 4d   Fig 4e

Assembling the Border

1 Measure from the top to the bottom of the quilt through the centre. This should be 42½in. Trim two 4½in cream strips to this length and stitch to each side of the quilt.

2 Measure across the quilt not including the border. This should be 34½in. Trim two 4½in cream strips to this length and sew a corner star block to each end of each one. Sew a strip to the top and bottom of the quilt (**Fig 5**).

Backing

Cut the backing fabric so that it is 2in larger than the quilt all the way round. Press any seams open. Cut the batting/wadding to the same size.

Quilting

1 Make the quilt sandwich of top, batting and backing and secure with safety pins, quilt tacks or basting spray if machine quilting, or by basting/tacking if hand sewing. (See Sewing Basics, page 16).

2 Quilt as desired. This quilt was quilted in the ditch with invisible/monofilament thread along most of the seams to stabilize the blocks. Then a multi-coloured thread was quilted in circles on the quarter-square triangle blocks with ribbons on the inner blocks and stippling around the outer blocks. The border was quilted with circles and swirls.

Binding and Finishing

1 Measure the perimeter of the quilt and join the 2½in mid-blue strips in a continuous piece to match your measurement, plus 3in.

2 Fold each strip in half along the length and press flat.

3 Refer to Sewing Basics, pages 17–19, for details on how to attach the binding, label and hanging sleeve.

Fig 5

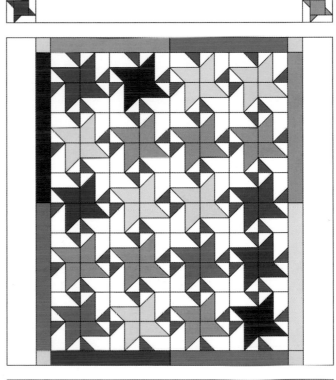

Triangles & Hexagons

On a recent trip to the north of England we discovered some outstanding marble floor tiles in Beverley Minster. The pattern made me realize how just a simple triangle can be made into wonderful tessellating designs and once I began to play with this one I found there were lots of patterns to be made. In the original floor tiles it is the hexagon made out of six triangles that dominates and it was this that I wanted to explore in more detail. As I worked on the quilts I was able to move away from the original inspiration to create a completely different look. The hexagon shape dominates in three of the quilts while the triangle itself was the inspiration for the other two. Instructions are given for two quilts in this chapter because there are two separate techniques for making them.

CAT'S CRADLE 47½ x 42in
Quilted by Rosemary Archer

The floor of Beverley Minster, near Hull, inspired this series of quilts.

Cat's Cradle

My starting point for this quilt was the hexagon shape. Drafting it out I became aware that I could create stars within the design by making separate hexagons and surrounding them with one colour. When the inner section of the quilt in bright yellow and dark blue cat fabric was cut, I chose the red fabric to become the inner stars. To contain the outer hexagons of turquoise and white cat fabric I needed a new colour that would also form a good frame. Bright green toned in with both cat fabrics and so more star shapes appeared as the quilt grew. The spotted black border harmonises with all the bright colours in the quilt. Keeping the quilt as a hexagon makes an unusual shape and will look really lively on a nursery wall. The yellow binding relates to the inner yellow triangles and adds another fun element to this quilt. Instructions for making Cat's Cradle begin on page 57.

BEVERLEY MOSAICS 48 x 57in
Quilted by Rosemary Archer

Beverley Mosaics

This is an almost exact replica of the original floor tiles from Beverley Minster – the original inspiration for this chapter. Hexagons are usually made up of three diamonds but in Beverley Minster, it is the triangle that makes the hexagon shape because of the placement of black, grey and white tiles. In this quilt, I chose a dark black and very dark grey for the main hexagons and a lighter grey and white for the secondary hexagons. The heavily marbled triangles on the original floor called for something a little different and I introduced some extra colour by using a mottled green, grey and pink batik. Once the triangles were pieced in horizontal rows, I framed them with a wide black sashing. I chose to accentuate the green and pink by making a magenta border of Flying Geese units laid side by side, which brought the quilt alive. A further row of black sashing and a dark grey binding add the final touch.

The triangles are arranged so that they create hexagons. We see the black and dark grey hexagons first, but then the green and grey hexagons appear and suddenly we can see hexagons everywhere.

53

Seaside Candy

SEASIDE CANDY 35 x 41in
Quilted by Pauline Blazey and Christine Porter

To re-create the design of Beverley Mosaics with hexagons in just two colours I chose a candy-striped pink and a cheerful turquoise, and filled in the remaining spaces with black triangles. Black six-pointed star shapes emerged, thus creating a completely new look. A further unexpected design also emerged – larger turquoise triangles with black centres alternating with pink triangles that also had black centres. More than one tessellating pattern in a quilt was too good to be true! I surrounded the inner part of the quilt with a white spotty fabric with a narrow sashing in the same fabric to make the tessellation look as though it is floating. A wider border of the black spotty fabric frames the quilt and as a final embellishment I stitched a frame of wide satin stitch in bright pink thread.

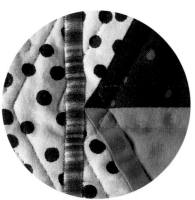

The satin-stitch border is worked in variegated thread, echoing the stripes on the pink fabric and picking up the colour of the dots on the turquoise and black fabrics.

Dolly Mixtures

DOLLY MIXTURES 55 x 54in
Quilted by Rosemary Archer

Triangles are grouped into four
to make a larger triangle that
uses two values of each colour.

I wanted to explore the tessellating larger triangle unit from Seaside Candy and found the ideal range of leafy fabrics in five colour ranges each in four different values from dark to light. I made up twenty different combinations of triangles using most of the fabrics in the range. As I laid them out on my cutting table, the fabrics reminded me of a favourite British sweet, Dolly Mixtures. As I pieced the triangle units I created diagonal lines of colour. I originally thought of cutting the sides straight, but as I looked again at the pattern I could see that the edges created another undulating tessellation, so I decided to keep it and fill in the edges with a border to make the inner design appear to float. With so many colours in this quilt, I chose a pale cream for this border, edged with a narrow sashing in the same colour. As a binding I chose a random selection of 15 colours and found that after I had pieced them, (also randomly) and sewed the binding on, almost all the colours are next to their own set of triangles – serendipity! Instructions for making Dolly Mixtures begin on page 61.

Starry, Starry Night

STARRY, STARRY NIGHT 57 x 64in
Quilted by Rosemary Archer

This quilt, in my favourite combination of blue and yellow, takes the tessellating triangles in quite another direction. Each unit has a pale central triangle and is surrounded with dark or medium blue strips, each of which has a yellow diamond on one end. When the resulting larger triangle units are joined in rows, six-pointed stars appear at the intersections. Having chosen a deep navy blue as the background to the large six-pointed star, there was some complex piecing to achieve the outer smaller yellow stars around it. Now dominant lines of small stars march both horizontally and diagonally across the quilt. I appliquéd four extra stars to the border at top and bottom to balance the quilt and surrounded the outside with a narrow strip of randomly pieced yellow, which also continues as the binding.

My large collection of blue striped and checked fabrics gives this the decorative look of a scrap quilt.

Cat's Cradle

Quilt Size: 47½ x 42in

MATERIALS

Fabric
100% cotton fabrics 44in wide:
- ½ yard each of turquoise, dark cats, light cats, bright red, bright green
- ¾ yard yellow
- 1 yard black with spots

Batting
52 x 48in

Backing
2 yards of your choice

Rulers
4½ x 12½in
Templates A, B and C (page 64) or buy one readymade from Creative Grids
Binding mitre tool with 120° angle (see Useful Addresses, page 120)

CUTTING

Measurements include ¼in seam allowances. Templates are given on page 64.

Dark cats
2 strips 3¾ x 44in. Cut into 21 of template A

Red
2 strips 3¾ x 44in. Cut into 24 of template A

Light cats
3 strips 3¾ x 44in. Cut into 36 of template A

Turquoise
3 strips 3¾ x 44in. Cut into 36 of template A

Green
2 strips 3¾ x 44in. Cut into 30 of template A

Don't forget to...

✔ Press the fabric before cutting. I use a fabric stabilizer or starch on the reverse side of the fabric. This makes for more accurate cutting, especially on long strips.

Black with spots (border)
- 1 strip 3¾ x 44in. Cut into 6 of template B
- 3 strips 3¾ x 44in. Cut into 12 of template C
- 6 strips 1¾ x 44in. Cut into 2 strips 24in; 2 strips 25½in and 2 strips 27in

Yellow
- 2 strips 3¾in x 44in. Cut into 21 of template A
- 6 strips 2½ x 38in for binding

Please note...

✔ To cut your triangles from the fabric strips, refer to Figs 1a, 1b and 1c.

Don't forget to...

✔ Use a design wall to help in the placement of the blocks. You can then stand back and judge the design before sewing, as you may wish to change some of the blocks around.

Fig 1a
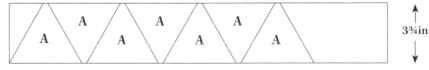
3¾in

Fig 1b
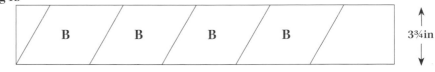
3¾in

Fig 1c

3¾in

QUILT DESIGN

Fig 2a

1 Place the blue cats and yellow triangles to form a hexagon (**Fig 2a**).

Fig 2b

2 Place 6 red triangles around the outside (**Fig 2b**).

Fig 2c

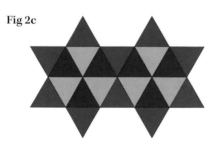

3 Add another hexagon of 3 yellow and 3 blue cat triangles surrounded by red triangles (**Fig 2c**).

Fig 2d

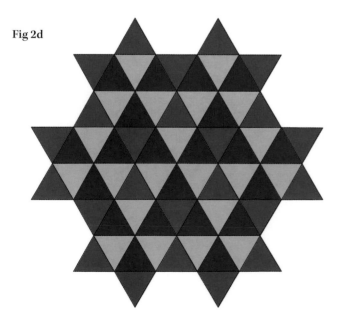

4 Continue to build up the pattern (**Figs 2d**).

Fig 2e

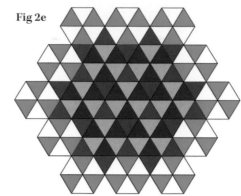

5 Around the outside place the white cat and turquoise triangles forming 12 further hexagons (**Fig 2e**).

6 Place the green triangles in the remaining gaps.

7 Now stand back and move the cat fabrics around within their colour groups until you have them facing the right way up, as far as you possibly can. You may have to cut some more to replace those cats that are just limbs and no heads, for example.

BLOCK ASSEMBLY

1 Starting with the top row, sew the triangles together (**Fig 3a**).

2 Continue with the remaining rows in the same way, pressing the seams towards the next triangle.

3 Sew the rows together. To match the rows, place a pin through the exact spot where the points of the triangles match, then put a pin either side (see below).

Fig 3a

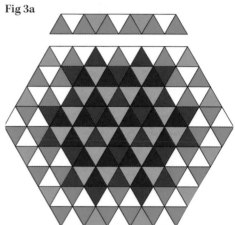

To prevent distortion…

✔ When sewing the rows together, first join the top five rows and then the last five rows. Now join them together. This helps prevent distortion.

Take care when sewing the rows together to use pins to match the exact places where the points of the triangles match, as shown below.

Adding the Border

1   Referring to **Fig 3b**, sew together two rows each of row A, B and C with the black border fabric cut with templates B and C, and the remaining green triangles (**Fig 3b**).

Fig 3c

Fig 3b

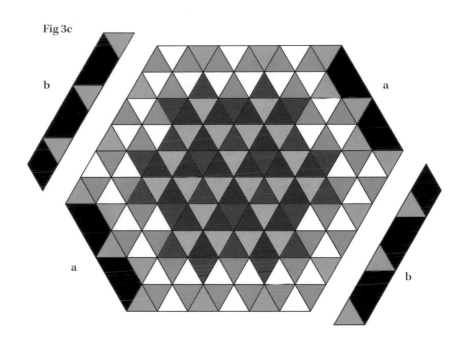

2   Sew row A on to two opposite sides of the quilt. Follow each row with row B, as shown (**Fig 3c**).

3   Sew row C on to the two remaining sides (**Fig 3d**).

4   Sew the 24in black strips on to two opposite sides. Press the border towards the edge. Trim off the excess at the corner by lining up the ruler with the adjacent side, as shown above.

5   Add the two 25½in black strips on to the two sides next to the ones you have just sewn and trim.

6   Sew the 27in black strips on to the remaining two sides and trim.

Fig 3d

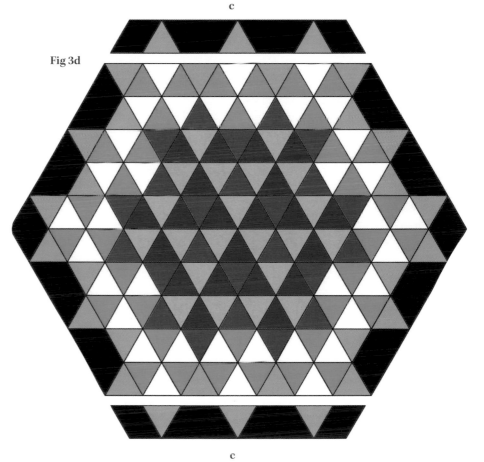

Backing

1   Cut the backing fabric 2in larger than the quilt all the way round.

2   Press any seams open.

3   Cut the batting/wadding to the same size.

QUILTING

1 Make the quilt sandwich of top, batting and backing and secure with safety pins, quilt tacks or basting spray if machine quilting, or by tacking if hand sewing. (See Sewing Basics, page 16.)

2 Quilt as desired. This quilt was quilted with geometric shapes including circles in the green triangles and at the centres of the hexagons and with ellipses in the border. Alternate hexagons have double flowers in the centres and the others have double sun shapes.

Binding and Finishing

1 Fold each 2½ x 38in yellow strip in half along the length and press flat.

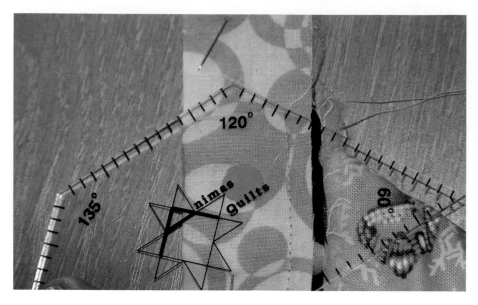

2 Sew one strip to each side of the quilt, stopping a bare ¼in from the ends, leaving a long tail at each end.

3 To mitre the corners, place two yellow tails together, matching exactly, and pin slightly away from the end and also before the end.

4 Place the Binding mitre tool across the yellow fabric and mark the angle, making sure you have an equal number of notches leading up to the point (see above).

5 Sew along the line.

6 Trim off the excess fabric, leaving only a small margin of fabric beyond the point so that the finished mitre will lie flat.

7 Turn the mitre through to the right side (see photo below).

8 Repeat for the other five corners.

9 Refer to Sewing Basics, pages 17–19, to complete the binding, and add the label and hanging sleeve. To allow this hexagonal quilt to hang flat you will need to make an additional 2in sleeve to place centrally across the back of the quilt in which to place a flat baton.

Don't forget to...

✔ Use a design wall to help with the placement of the blocks. Stand back and judge the design before sewing as you may wish to change some of the blocks around. (See Sewing Basics, page 10.)

Quilt Size: 55 x 54in

MATERIALS

Fabric
100% cotton fabrics 44in wide:
• ¼ yard of a range of dark green to light green (4), brown to pale yellow (4), red to pink (4), purple to lavender (4), dark blue to pale blue (5). Alternatively, use at least four different fabrics divided between dark, medium and light in each of five colour ranges.
• 1¾ yards cream

Batting
60 x 60in

Backing
3 yards of your choice

Rulers
2½ x 12½in
4½ x 12½in
Templates A and D
(page 64)

Dolly Mixtures

CUTTING
Measurements include ¼in seam allowances. Templates are given on page 64.

Green
Dark: 1 strip (3¾in wide) cut into 8 triangles using template A
Dark/medium: 2 strips (3¾in wide) cut into 24 triangles using template A
Medium: 2 strips (3¾in wide) cut into 20 triangles using template A
Light: 3 strips (3¾in wide) cut into 44 triangles using template A

Brown
Dark: 1 strip (3¾in wide) cut into 7 triangles using template A
Medium: 2 strips (3¾in wide) cut into 27 triangles using template A
Yellow: 2 strips (3¾in wide) cut into 20 triangles using template A
Pale yellow/cream: 1 strip (3¾in wide) cut into 14 triangles using template A

Red
Dark: 2 strips (3¾in wide) cut into 23 triangles using template A
Dark/medium: 1 strip (3¾in wide) cut into 15 triangles using template A
Medium: 2 strips (3¾in wide) cut into 24 triangles using template A
Light pink: 1 strip (3¾in wide) cut into 10 triangles using template A

Don't forget to…

✔ Press the fabric before cutting. I use a fabric stabilizer or starch on the reverse side of the fabric. This makes for more accurate cutting, especially on long strips.

Purple
Dark: 2 strips (3¾in wide) cut into 17 triangles using template A
Dark/medium: 2 strips (3¾in wide) cut into 16 triangles using template A
Medium: 2 strips (3¾in wide) cut into 27 triangles using template A
Light: 2 strips (3¾in wide) cut into 24 triangles using template A

Cream
4 strips (7 x 44in) cut into 16 triangles using template D for the border
2 strips (2 x 52½in) for the border (see the tip, top right), joining pieces as necessary
2 strips (2 x 55¾in) for the border (see the tip, top right), joining pieces as necessary

15 assorted colours
From each cut:
1 strip (2½ x 18in) for binding

For accuracy…

✔ Don't cut out the border strips until you have assembled the main part of the quilt. Then measure the quilt and cut the border strips to fit. This way your border will fit neatly even if your quilt is not quite the same size as mine.

Refer to Fig 1 below to cut your triangles from the fabric strips.

Fig 1

3¾in

UNIT ASSEMBLY

1 Sew a medium brown triangle to each edge of a dark brown triangle (**Row 1**). This is one unit (**Fig 2**).

Fig 2

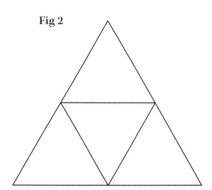

2 Referring to **Fig 3a**, make up the following colour combinations:

• 2 units of pale green around dark/medium green (**Row 2a**).

• 3 units of dark/medium purple around pale lavender (**Row 2b**).

• 4 units of dark blue around medium blue (**Row 3a**).

• 5 units of dark/medium red around pale pink (**Row 3b**).

• 6 units of yellow around dark/medium brown (**Row 4a**).

• 7 units of dark/medium green around pale green (**Row 4b**).

• 8 units of medium purple around dark purple (**Row 5a**).

• 8 units of medium blue around pale blue (**Row 5b**).

• 8 units of medium green around dark green (**Row 6a**).

• 8 units of medium brown around pale yellow/cream (**Row 6b**).

• 8 units of medium pink around dark red (**Row 7a**).

• 8 units of dark/medium blue around medium blue (**Row 7b**).

• 7 units of pale lavender around dark/medium purple (**Row 8a**).

• 6 units of dark/medium green around pale green (**Row 8b**).

• 5 units of dark red around pale pink (**Row 9a**).

• 4 units of pale blue around medium blue (**Row 9b**).

• 3 units of dark purple around medium purple (**Row 10a**).

• 2 units of pale yellow/cream around yellow (**Row 10b**).

• 1 unit of dark/medium green around pale green (**Row 11**).

QUILT ASSEMBLY

1 Place the medium brown/dark brown unit for row 1 on the design wall at the top left-hand side.

2 Place the other triangles on the wall row by row (**Fig 3a**).

3 Sew two cream triangles, D, to the appropriate end of rows 1, 2, 3, 4, 8, 9, 10 and 11 (**Fig 3b**).

Fig 3a

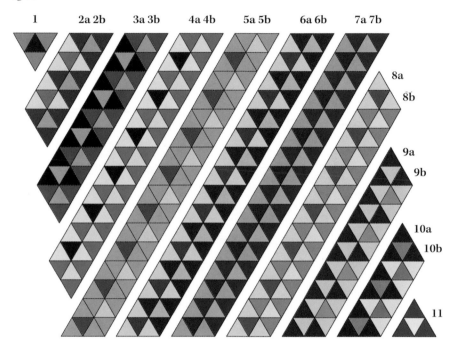

Fig 3b

4 Join the rows together.

5 Trim the quilt into a rectangle
   (**Fig 3c**) by laying a large ruler along
   each cream edge, leaving a good ¼in
   seam allowance along the edge.

7 Sew one 2 x 52½in strip of cream
   fabric to each side of the quilt using
   white thread. Press outwards.

8 Sew one 2 x 55¾in strip of cream
   fabric to the top and bottom of the
   quilt (**Fig 3d**).

9 Press the seams outwards.

Backing

1 Cut the backing fabric 2in larger
   all round than the quilt. Press any
   seams open.

2 Cut the batting/wadding to the
   same size.

Quilting

1 Make the quilt sandwich of top,
   batting and backing and secure with
   safety pins, quilt tacks or basting
   spray if machine quilting, or by
   basting/tacking if hand sewing. (See
   Sewing Basics, page 16.)

2 Quilt as desired. This quilt was
   quilted in diagonal lines with a
   fantasy leaf design in variegated
   thread. The border features a
   complementary feather design in
   cream on cream.

Binding and Finishing

1 Measure the perimeter of the quilt
   and join the 18 x 2½in strips of
   different colours in a continuous
   piece to fit, plus 3in. (See Sewing
   Basics, page 17.)

2 Fold the strip in half along the
   length and press flat.

3 Refer to Sewing Basics, pages 17–19,
   for details on how to attach the
   binding, label and hanging sleeve.

Fig 3c

Fig 3d

Templates

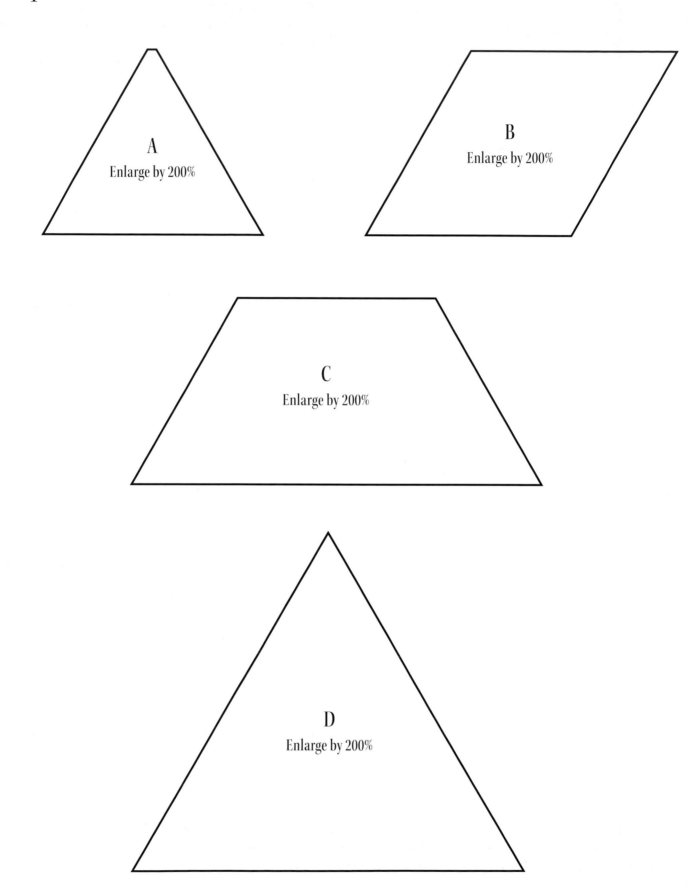

A
Enlarge by 200%

B
Enlarge by 200%

C
Enlarge by 200%

D
Enlarge by 200%

Creative Options

The easiest way to quilt is usually in straight lines, following or echoing the lines of the seams. This is excellent for beginners and usually produces subtle but pleasing results. However, stitching in swirls, leafy or feathery patterns provides a change of pace and adds an appealing touch. Remember to stitch in the ditch first, using invisible/monofilament thread, to stabilize the quilt before any additional quilting.

STARRY. STARRY NIGHT Rosemary Archer used yellow variegated cotton to quilt wonderful whimsical feathers over the dark border of this quilt and she continued this theme across the centre. Curling vines in yellow, radiating out from the middle of the yellow stars, echo the design on the feathers in the border for a pleasing harmony. These elements add an ornate, decorative touch to the otherwise stark geometry of the quilt and ensure that there is a feast for the eye.

BEVERLEY MOSAICS Here the quilting stitches both enforce the strong geometry of the piecing and soften it. The circles in the hexagons and spiralling ovals in the border continue the geometrical theme yet introduce new and exciting shapes, while the wreaths of oak leaves around the grey and black hexagons have a definite softening effect.

DOLLY MIXTURES Here the quilting stitches follow the diagonal design of the quilt but in a pretty leaf and frond design that adds to the intricate look of the quilt, and contributes to the overall effect of busy activity. A complementary feather design is used in the border to complete the look.

Diamonds

I was pleased to find a good example of a tessellating pattern almost on my doorstep – a nearby gate decorated in a set of white diamonds that were separated by thick black lines. As with any tessellated design the interlocking shapes can go on into infinity and only stop when a border is drawn to prevent the design from going any further.

The gate is black and white but I quickly recognized the possibilities for playing with colour. There would also be opportunities to use different techniques to outline the diamonds using bias binding, ribbon or rickrack braid. These were my final choices but there are many other possibilities you could use.

SATURDAY MARKET 58½ x 47in
Quilted by Rosemary Archer

Saturday Market

Using my Diamond template (see page 71), I cut the diamonds so that I could display this collection of fruit and vegetable fabrics to good advantage and cut three of each fabric except the carrots, which required four pieces. I made sure that as I placed the basic colours across the quilt I also separated the individual designs and as far as possible avoided putting them on the same diagonal. This gives the impression that the pieces are randomly scattered across the quilt. The light green border allows the diamonds to 'float' and also ties all the colours together. Instructions for making Saturday Market begin on page 71.

This unusual gate inspired a whole series of quilts.

66

GIVERNY FANTASY 32 x 62in
By Sally Ablett

Giverny Fantasy

Giverny was Monet's home, where he spent much of his time in the garden and painted many an iris and water lily, so it is easy to see where this quilt gets its name. The quilt was made by Sally Ablett, who combined the design of the gate with a stunning range of fabrics from Woodrow Studio, called Wings of Desire. This quilt is an exact replica of the gate, made of four full diamonds both across and down, the only difference being that the quilt hangs vertically rather than horizontally. The effect is like a stained-glass window: the tall, thin format is the window recess and the black rickrack braid, sashing and binding are the leading. The wonderful variegated fabric of the border is the final touch, capturing the effect of light through coloured glass.

The quilt stitching captures the essence of Monet's garden: water, plants and flowers.

White Christmas

WHITE CHRISTMAS 56½ x 54in
Quilted by Sally Ablett

Using the diamond template, I decided to challenge myself to make a pictorial quilt. White Christmas was the result and I had fun working out this tree design with a limited palette. I also challenged myself not to buy any extra fabric and managed to find various white and gold pieces for the background in my collection. The four corner diamonds were each made of 9 smaller diamonds and the border was designed with an equal number of dark red and dark green gold striped fabric rectangles. Gold fusible bias tape outlined the diamonds on the tree for a festive look. I then embellished it with cheerful baubles at the intersections of the diamonds within the tree and added gold and dark green tinsel using a zigzag stitch for an extra Holiday Season effect.

A heavy white rayon thread was used to add lively stars and squiggles to the background, while wavy lines of gold stitching embellish the border strips.

Gathering the Grapes

GATHERING THE GRAPES 35½ x 46in
Quilted by Kathy Sandbach

Inspired by the border fabric of grapes and vines, I picked out many different coordinating tones of green, mauve and yellow/orange. I cut several diamonds in each fabric for the design phase and scattered them randomly across the interior of the quilt. Once I was happy with the arrangement, I sewed the diamonds together and outlined them using a deep purple ribbon. Next I appliquéd small rectangles of orange and purple grapes at the intersections. The dark border and dark purple binding frame the lantern shapes, helping to draw the eye in.

Stitched grape and leaf designs reinforce the theme of the quilt.

Lavender Dream

LAVENDER DREAM 60 x 62in
Quilted by Rosemary Archer

While designing Saturday Market, I inadvertently misplaced some diamonds on the design wall and found that I had made a chevron pattern. This gave me the idea of creating Lavender Dream. To create the three-dimensional illusion I needed 30 different fabrics! There are two distinct vertical rows, one light and the other dark, each having fourteen fabrics. I made eight sets of these two rows and then joined them together to make the quilt. The borders are made up of light lavender and dark purple with a binding of dark purple.

This design relies for its success on the placement of tones.

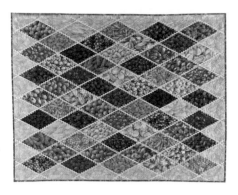

Saturday Market

Quilt Size: 58½ x 47½in

MATERIALS

Fabric
100% cotton fabrics 44in wide:
• ⅛ yard of 22 assorted themed bright fabrics
• 1⅛ yard pale green
• ½ yard dark green

Batting
64 x 52in

Backing
2½ yards your choice

Rulers
6½ x 12½in
Diamond template A (right)
or buy a clear plastic version
(see Useful Addresses,
page 120)

Don't forget to...

✔ Use a design wall to help in the placement of the blocks. You can then stand back and judge the design before sewing, as you may wish to change some of the blocks around. (See Sewing Basics, page 10.)

CUTTING

Measurements include ¼in seam allowances.

22 assorted fabrics
⅛ yard. Cut into 3 diamonds using template A and in one fabric cut an extra diamond

Pale green
• 5 strips (6⅛ x 44in). Cut into 24 diamonds
• 5 strips (2 x 44in) for the border

Dark green
5 strips (2½ x 44in) for the binding

Please note...

✔ Diagrams show the fabric pieces without seam allowances for clarity.

BLOCK ASSEMBLY

1 Place the assorted diamonds on your design wall, making sure there is plenty of contrast between them so that the individual colours stand out (**Fig 1a**).

Fig 1a

To cut the diamonds from fabric strips, lay your template in place as shown.

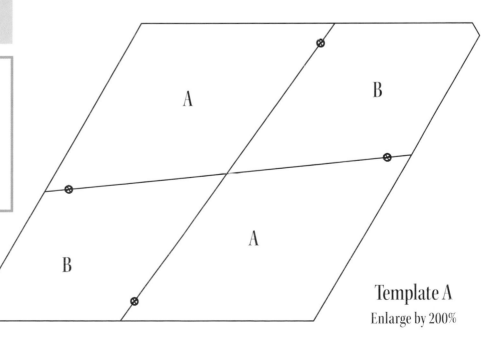

A

B

B

A

Template A
Enlarge by 200%

Fig 1b

2   Continue to fill in the diamonds until you have seven rows of five alternating with six rows of four (**Fig 1b**).

3   Add the pale green diamonds around the edges (**Fig 1c**).

4   Sew the diamonds together in diagonal rows (**Fig 1d**).

Fig 1c

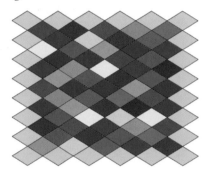

Fig 1d

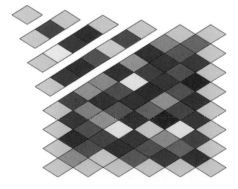

5   Press the seams in each row in alternate directions so that when you sew the rows together the points can match without too much bulk.

6   Sew the rows together.

Adding the Border

1   Use a large square and a long ruler to trim and square up the quilt (**Fig 2a**).

Fig 2a

2   Make sure there is a generous ¼in beyond each point before cutting.

3   Sew the long pale green 2in strips into one long continuous strip (see Sewing Basics, page 17).

4   Measure the width across the centre and also across the top and bottom. Cut two 2in strips that long. Mine measured 56½in.

5   Sew the strips along the top and bottom of the quilt and press outwards.

6   Measure the length down the centre of the quilt from top to bottom and at both side edges. Cut two 2in strips to that measurement. Mine measured 48½in.

7   Sew the strips to the sides of the quilt and press outwards (**Fig 2b**).

Fig 2b

For a perfect match…

✔ When attaching long narrow strips, fold each strip in half and mark the fold with a pin. Fold the quilt in half and mark with a pin too. Match up the two centre pins and pin the two outer edges together exactly. Now place more pins along the edges, easing gently, if necessary.

Backing

1   Cut the backing fabric 2in larger than the quilt all the way round.

2   Press any seams open.

3   Cut the batting/wadding to the same size.

Quilting

1   Make the quilt sandwich of top, batting and backing and secure with safety pins, quilt tacks or basting spray if machine quilting, or by basting/tacking if hand sewing. (See Sewing Basics, page 16.)

2   Quilt as desired. For Saturday Market, yellow rickrack braid was applied across the quilt in rows to outline the diamonds and to stop the fruit and vegetables blending into each other. Variegated thread in red, orange and yellow was used to quilt circles on the diamonds and leafy feathers in the border.

Binding and Finishing

1   Measure the perimeter of the quilt and join the 2½in dark green strips in a continuous strip to match the perimeter of the quilt, plus 3in.

2   Fold each strip in half along the length and iron flat.

3   Refer to Sewing Basics, pages 17–19, for details on how to attach the binding and hanging sleeve.

Creative Options

Some designs work really well when finished with a trimming of ribbon, braid or satin stitch, and this design is a prime example. I've tended to use ribbon or braid because it is quick and easy to apply and you can lay it on your fabric before you stitch to see exactly what effect you'll achieve, but stitching would work too.

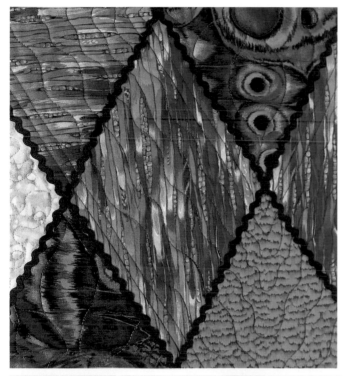

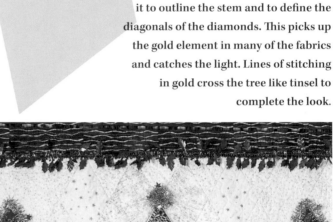

GIVERNY FANTASY This design looks so much like a stained-glass window, and it is the black rickrack braid that helps achieve that effect. It also emphasizes the diamond pattern while at the same time softening the hard edges of the design.

WHITE CHRISTMAS I applied fusible gold bias tape to the Christmas tree here, using it to outline the stem and to define the diagonals of the diamonds. This picks up the gold element in many of the fabrics and catches the light. Lines of stitching in gold cross the tree like tinsel to complete the look.

GATHERING THE GRAPES Here I outlined the diamond pattern with purple ribbon, couching it on by machine and sewing down the diagonal lines. I finished the edges of the rectangular blocks in black satin stitch to match the fabric.

Pine Bark

Some years ago I went to a small exhibition in a quilt shop in Berkeley, California where a quilt made by Ann Ito caught my eye. It was an intricate tessellating design based on a diamond shape with sharp razor edges. Drafting the design later proved difficult and I could see that I needed a template to help with accurate cutting. It was necessary to divide the sides of the diamond into small symmetrical shapes that produced two kite shapes and two slightly offset diamonds.

Piecing the shapes together to form the tessellation was an interesting exercise and the instructions for making Polka Dot Ragtime (page 79), are the result of many attempts to come up with the easiest and most accurate way of creating this design. I have since discovered that this design is called the Pine Bark pattern and is seen in Japanese Sashiko designs.

POLKA DOT RAGTIME 35¼ x 35¼in

Polka Dot Ragtime

This is my favourite Pine Bark quilt. I love to collect themed fabrics, and here I was able to utilize my stash of bright and colourful polka dots. You will only need a fat quarter or ⅛ yard of each of the 23 colours but I always find it helpful to cut additional fabric because it provides more options at the design wall stage. The idea is to place each fabric so that no one colour is near itself and there are no repeats. The black border sets off the bright colours of the interior and for the binding I wanted something that links back to the main colours. I was lucky enough to find exactly the right spotty binding, which combines all the colours on a black background. Instructions for making this quilt begin on page 79.

The fabrics in a quilt can have any kind of linking theme. It doesn't have to be colour. Here, for example, dots are the unifying factor.

CHRISTMAS LANTERNS 61 x 42in

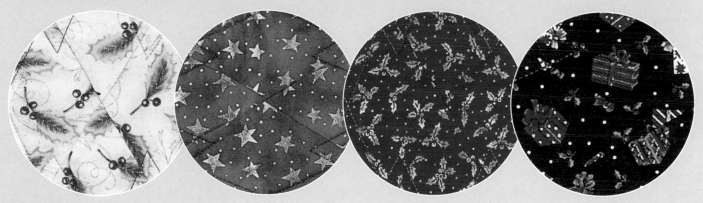

Christmas Lanterns

I wanted a wall hanging to put up over the Christmas period and this quilt gave me a good excuse to attack my stash of Christmas fabrics. Still using the large diamond template, I cut around 50 different fabrics based on green, red, cream and black. In the end I used 41 fabrics for this quilt, balancing the darker colours with several carefully placed fabrics that had pale backgrounds. These lighten the overall effect and help to keep the mid tones bright and clear. The wide, star-studded border frames the colourful centre and makes it seem as if the diamond shapes are floating. As a finishing touch, the festive quilt is framed by a green binding with a seasonal design of red poinsettias.

The medley of Christmas-themed fabrics creates a feast for the eye.

Run Rabbit Run

RUN RABBIT RUN 66½ x 50in

Batik fabrics in turquoise, mulberry and green with a few others for extra interest are the basis of this zingy quilt. I used 50 different batiks but I had many more on my design wall before I decided on the final arrangement of diamonds. As I built up the formation I realized that I did not have enough of the black hand-dyed fabric I had planned for the border. Undaunted I decided to turn necessity to advantage and added a darker greyish black fabric going to the edge. Outlining the change between these fabrics is a bright ribbon, which I couched onto the seam. The final shape of the quilt was determined by the amount of the outer black fabric – there was not enough to square off the corners. I like the effect, but more sleeves were required across the corners on the back to make the quilt hang correctly.

Sometimes batik fabrics are so bright that they leap out at you from the shelves. As you see, they can work brilliantly together.

Coral Waves

CORAL WAVES 31½ x 21½in

This design utilizes smaller shapes created by placing the marking holes in a slightly different position on the edges. This also creates a slightly different shape. I chose 18 contrasting values in pink and blue to make this small wall hanging. The elongated shapes seem to float along like waves, with the wide, dark pink batik border emphasizing this effect. The sparkling binding fabric looks as though the sun is glistening on the waves and pulls the piece together.

Using fabrics that share the same colours – blues with pinks or pinks with blues – helps ensure an overall harmony.

Treasure Trove

TREASURE TROVE 26½ x 35½in

This variation of Coral Waves is hung vertically, giving it a whole new look, like a flying carpet from Aladdin's cave. I picked out 18 sumptuous fabrics in red, green, brown, black and blue to form the interior of the quilt and used the smaller template to create an elongated look. The black surrounding the colourful diamonds brings out their ornate richness and separates the sparkling gold border. I added more black beyond the gold and this time attached a matching black binding because I didn't want to draw the eye away from the bejewelled interior.

Many of the fabrics have gold patterning, which adds to the opulent effect.

Polka Dot Ragtime

Quilt Size: 35¼ x 35¼in

MATERIALS

Fabric
100% cotton fabrics 44in wide:
• ⅛ yard of 30 contrasting polka dot fabrics in pink, green, yellow, blue, orange, purple and turquoise from which to choose a final 23
• 1 yard black
• ¼ yard bright polka dots on black for binding

Batting
40in square

Backing
1⅛ yards of your choice

Rulers
2½ x 12½in
Diamond Template (right) or buy a clear plastic version (see Useful Addresses, page 120)

Extras
Marking pen or pencil for light and dark fabrics

> **Don't forget to...**
>
> ✔ Use a design wall to help in the placement of the blocks. You can then stand back and judge the design.

CUTTING
Measurements include ¼in seam allowances.

Polka dot fabric
Cut a diamond from each polka dot fabric and make a dot through the holes along the outer edges of the template with the fabric marker. Carefully remove the diamond template. Place a ruler diagonally across the fabric between dots and cut the diamond in two. Now place the ruler along the opposite diagonal and cut the diamond again, making four pieces in total, two like off-set diamonds, A, and two like kites, B (**Fig 1a**).

Black
• 12 diamonds from the template, cutting each one into four as for the polka dot fabrics
• 2 strips (4 x 29in)
• 2 strips (4 x 36in)

Binding
4 strips (2½ x 44in)

> **Please note...**
>
> ✔ Diagrams show the fabric pieces without seam allowances for clarity.

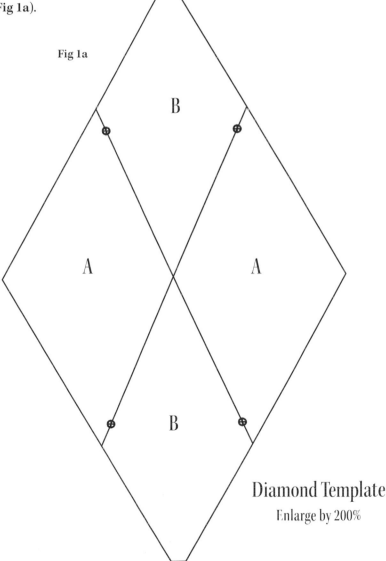

Fig 1a

Diamond Template
Enlarge by 200%

QUILT DESIGN

1   Keeping the four pieces of each fabric in their own piles, align the fabrics in a row on a table or ironing board next to the design wall to make it easy to select your colours.

2   Take one colour and place it on the design wall in the top left-hand corner, flipping each piece through 180°. The offset diamonds, A, have a shallow side and a deeper side that goes to the middle. The kites (**B**) face outwards (**Fig 1a**).

3   Build up the design, adding the fabrics four pieces at a time (**Fig 1b**).

4   Continue in this way until you have 23 fabrics that look good together with plenty of contrast between the colours (**Fig 1c**).

5   Try to arrange the lighter fabrics on the outer edges so they will contrast with the dark background.

6   Fill the edges with the black background shapes, A and B, taking care to keep the kites and offset diamonds in the correct places (**Fig 1d**).

BLOCK ASSEMBLY

1   Join the first set of pieces at the top left-hand corner in pairs and then join the pairs to make the original diamond shape (**Fig 2a**).

2   Add the two black side pieces to complete row A (**Fig 2b**).

3   Still referring to **Fig 2b**, assemble row B by sewing the kites and offset diamonds together as for row A, adding the outer black pieces last. Continue for the remaining rows.

4   Sew the rows together to make one large piece, taking care to match the centres of the Pine Bark motifs. Press the seams open or to one side.

5   To straighten the edges, use a long ruler to mark a chalk line on the right side along the outer edges.

Fig 1a

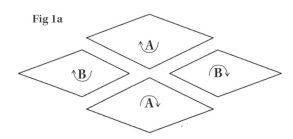

Pieces rotated 180°

Fig 1b

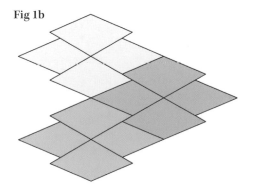

Fig 1c

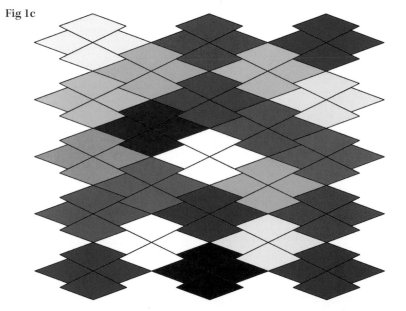

Fig 1d

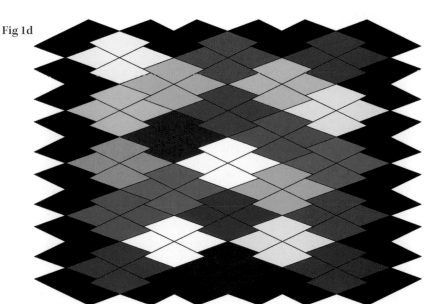

Fig 2a

The line should be ¼in from the tops of the points of the Pine Bark motifs. Place the ruler ⅛in over the chalk line to give yourself leeway when stitching on the border so that you do not cut off the points; cut along the edge of the ruler.

Fig 2b

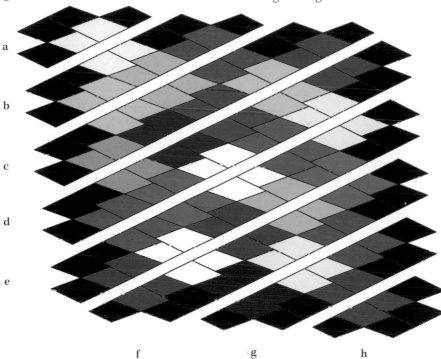

a

b

c

d

e

f   g   h

Fig 3

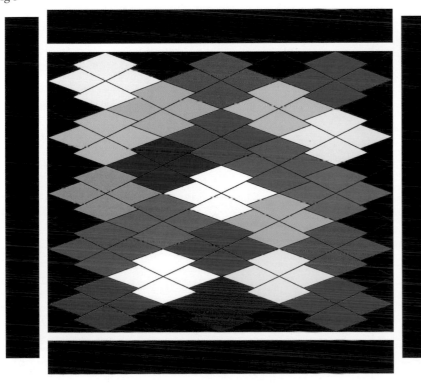

To help prevent distortion...

✔ When attaching the rows, first join rows A, B, C and D. Now make another set by joining E, F, G and H. Finally join the two sets together. This helps prevent distortion.

Adding the Border

1 Sew the two 4 x 29in black strips to the top and bottom of the quilt (**Fig 3**).

2 Press the seams outwards.

3 Sew the two 4 x 36in black strips to the remaining sides of the quilt. Press the seams outwards.

Quilting

1 Cut the backing fabric 2in larger than the quilt top all the way round. Press any seams open. Cut the batting/wadding to the same size.

2 Make the quilt sandwich of top, batting and backing and secure with safety pins, quilt tacks or basting spray if machine quilting, or by tacking if hand sewing. (See Sewing Basics, page 16.)

3 Quilt as desired. This quilt was quilted in straight lines inside the Pine Bark motifs, matching the thread to the different colours. The border was quilted in zigzag lines in metallic thread, echoing the outer lines.

Binding and Finishing

1 Measure the perimeter of the quilt and join the four 2½in wide strips in a continuous piece to match your measurement, plus 3in (see Sewing Basics, page 17).

2 Fold each strip in half along the length and press flat.

3 Refer to Sewing Basics, pages 17–19, for details on how to attach the binding and hanging sleeve.

T Block

I have long been interested in all things Oriental and have been fortunate to visit the East several times. On my return from one of these visits I made a quilt based on Marge Burkell's Kimono Medley, and as I was piecing the Kimono blocks I was reminded of traditional American quilts I had seen based on a T-shaped block. Once I began I soon found that the blocks tessellated, so my Oriental inspiration had led to another series of quilts.

The interesting thing about this design is that the tessellation of the T blocks gives a very emphatic positive and negative space. It is also one of the few tessellations that is an actual square block.

ORIENTAL KIMONOS 39 x 39in
Quilted by Rosemary Archer

Oriental Kimonos

For this quilt I chose a basic design of 16 blocks and theme colours of red, black and grey, alternating the colours with cream T-blocks to highlight the positive and negative spaces. Since there were designs on the fabrics that I wanted to feature, I decided to 'fussy cut' the body of the T using a plastic template (see the tip on page 87). I chose a rich red and gold fabric for the border and continued the fabric theme by using a black and gold fabric with Oriental characters for the binding. Instructions for making this quilt begin on page 87.

The kimono block that reminded me of the American T block.

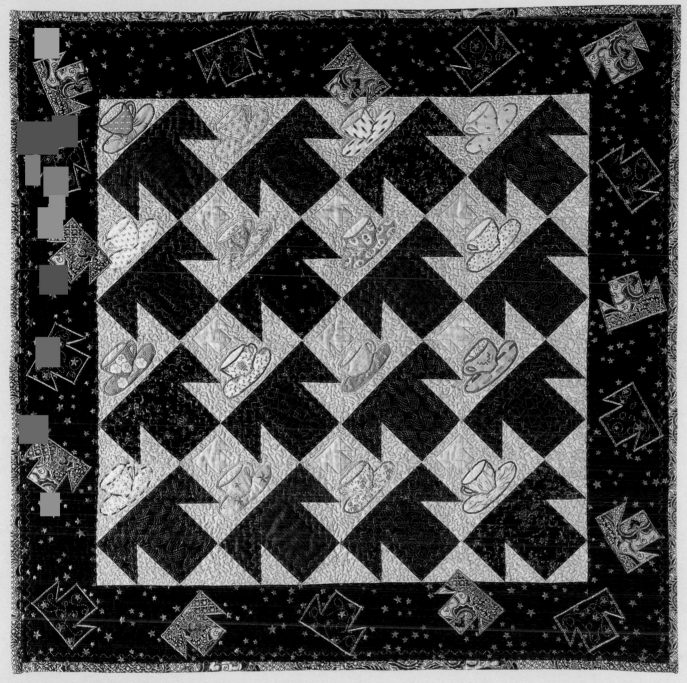

TEA TIME 32 x 32in

Tea Time

This quilt was made as a progression from the first quilt with a definite difference between the black Ts and the yellow background Ts. Six black and gold fabrics werc used for the 16 dark blocks and I used the black with gold stars for the border. I found some tiny floral prints for the teacups and saucers and made a plastic template as a cutting aid. I fused the fabric shapes on to the quilt and edged them all with a fine satin stitch. Then I made a smaller plastic template of the T shapc and, using an unusual Indonesian gold embellished fabric, I cut out and fused several shapes randomly around the border and outlined them with gold satin stitch.

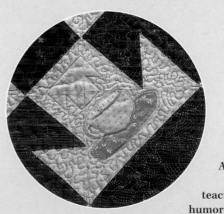

Appliquéd Ts and teacups add a humorous twist.

Folk – Dancing

FOLK – DANCING 39 x 39in
Quilted by Rosemary Archer

Here I wanted to experiment with using different colours in the negative space. I found a fun fabric with dancing figures on it and picked out yellow, green, turquoise, dark pink and orange for the background. Using the 'fussy cutting' technique, (see the tip on page 87), I laid my template exactly over the little figures to centre one in each T block. I framed the inner quilt with black and chose a bright starry fabric for the border with a primary colour striped binding to make a perfect ending.

With a large design fussy cutting ensures perfect results.

Butterfly Symphony

BUTTERFLY SYMPHONY 46 x 47in
Quilted by Rosemary Archer

In this quilt I gave myself the challenge of using just two colours. I wanted to experiment with changing values and chose as many fabrics as I could in both colours to go from the very palest through to the darkest. The turquoise acts as the background and starts at its very palest from the border, getting darker towards the centre. The pinks, which are the positive T blocks, go in the opposite direction, giving the impression of frames, one inside the other. I used a simple method to piece the 49 T blocks, which is explained on page 89.

The differences between fabrics of each tone are often subtle. This draws the viewer in to examine the quilt in detail.

International T Block

INTERNATIONAL T BLOCK 46 x 46in
Made by Tracey Brookshier, USA

This attractive T block quilt has an international flavour because Tracey used fabric from America, France and Britain. A collection of contrasting blues and yellows ranging from light to dark values gives this quilt quite a different look to the first three as there is no single background colour. The Ts facing downwards are mostly in shades of yellow, while the Ts facing upwards are mostly in shades of blue, which gives a good contrast and adds interest.

The wide border, narrower sashing and then even finer sashing help to draw the eye of the viewer in towards the centre of the quilt.

Quilt Size: 39 x 39in

MATERIALS

Fabric
A variety of 100% cotton fabrics 44in wide:
• ⅛ yard (fat) each of 16 contrasting fabrics with an Oriental theme
• 1 yard marbled cream for the background
• ¾ yard dark red stripe for the border
• ½ yard black and gold for binding

Batting
43 x 43in

Backing
1½ yards of your choice

Ruler
18½ x 6½in

Extras
• 1 sheet heavy template plastic
• Fine permanent marker pen

Oriental Kimonos

CUTTING
Measurements include ¼in seam allowances.

16 contrast fabrics
From each cut:
• 1 square (4⅜in) cut in half on the diagonal to make 2 triangles (C)
• 1 piece A (see the tip, right) using template A, below

Marbled cream
• 4 strips (44 x 3⅜in). Cut each into 12 squares (3⅜in) and cut in half on the diagonal to make 80 triangles (B)
• 2 strips (44 x 5⅞in). Cut into 8 squares (5⅞in) and cut each one in half on the diagonal to make 16 triangles (D)

Dark red stripe
4 strips (5 x 40in) for the border

Black and gold
4 strips 44 x 2½in wide for binding

To fussy cut...
✔ Trace template A on to template plastic with a permanent marker pen and then place your new template over each contrasting fabric. Move it around until you can frame a pleasing section of the design or even a whole motif. Now cut out the piece carefully. It does not matter if the fabric is slightly on the bias.

Template A

Actual Size

BLOCK ASSEMBLY

BLOCK 1

Finished block size 7½in square

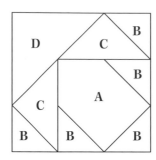

1. For each block sew one B triangle (background fabric) to each side of the matching A piece. Stitch a B triangle in the remaining corner (**Fig 1a**).
2. Sew a B triangle to the right-hand side of one triangle C (**Fig 1b**).
3. Sew a B triangle to the left-hand side of the remaining triangle C (**Fig 1c**).

Fig 1a   **Fig 1b**   **Fig 1c**

4. Sew these two pieces to the square as shown in **Fig 1d**.
5. Sew the D triangle (background fabric) to the top of the T, completing one block (**Fig 1e**).
6. Make up 16 T blocks altogether in this way.

Fig 1d   **Fig 1e**

Fig 2

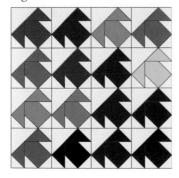

Assembling the Quilt

1. Lay the blocks out in four rows of four blocks in colour combinations of your choice.
2. Sew the blocks together in four horizontal rows and then join the rows together (**Fig 2**).

Adding the Borders

1. Measure the length of the quilt through the centre. It should be 30in plus the outer seam allowances.
2. Fold the four dark red border strips in half to find the centre and mark with a pin.
3. Measure 5in from each end of each border strip and mark with a pin.
4. Measure 15in (half the length of the quilt) along each side of the quilt and mark with a pin.
5. Lay one border strip over one edge of the quilt with right sides facing, matching the two centre pins and positioning the pins at each end of the border at the edge of the quilt (**Fig 3a**).
6. Stitch the strip in place.
7. Repeat to sew the other border strips to the remaining three sides of the quilt.
8. Mitre the ends of the border strips as explained in Sewing Basics, page 14 (**Fig 3b**).
9. Press the border to the outside.

Fig 3a

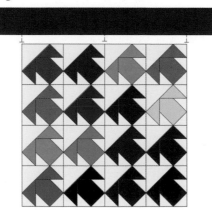

Fig 3b

Backing

1. Cut the backing fabric 2in larger all round than the quilt.
2. Press any seams open.
3. Cut the batting/wadding to the same size.

Quilting

1. Make the quilt sandwich of top, batting and backing and secure with safety pins, quilt tacks or basting spray if machine quilting, or by basting/tacking if hand sewing. (See Sewing Basics, page 16.)
2. Quilt as desired. This quilt was quilted in the ditch along most of the seams to stabilize the blocks. A pine bark motif was quilted around the inner blocks with stippling around the outer blocks. Wavy lines were quilted on the red border stripe.

Binding and Finishing

1. Measure the perimeter of the quilt and join the 2½in black strips in a continuous strip to match your measurement, plus 3in.
2. Fold each strip in half along the length and press flat.
3. Refer to Sewing Basics, pages 17–19, for details on how to attach the binding, label and hanging sleeve.

Alternative Block

If you don't need to fussy cut the T shape you can make your T blocks as explained here. This is an easier method because it is based on strip piecing.

CUTTING

16 contrasting fabrics

From each cut:

• 1 strip 3⅜ x 10½in. Cut into 3 squares (3⅜in)

• 1 square (5⅞in). Cut in half on the diagonal. (You will only use one of these triangles)

Marbled cream

• 4 strips 3⅜ x 44in. Cut into 40 squares (3⅜in)

• 8 squares (5⅞in). Cut each in half on the diagonal

BLOCK ASSEMBLY

Finished size 6in square

1 Draw a line through the diagonal on the back of all the 3⅜in cream squares.

2 Place a cream square on top of a contrasting 3⅜in square and sew ¼in each side of the marked line (**Fig 4a**). Cut along the marked line.

3 Press the two squares open (**Fig 4b**).

4 Make five squares in this way for each colour of contrasting fabric.

5 Draw a line through the diagonal on the back of all the 5⅞in cream squares.

6 Place a large cream triangle on top of a large contrasting triangle and sew together along the diagonal.

7 Press each square open with seams pressed towards the darker fabric.

8 Join two small squares and sew on to the large square. Join two smaller squares and add a further square facing in the opposite direction (**Fig 4c**).

Fig 4a

Fig 4b

9 Sew the three joined squares to the rest of the block (**Fig 4d**).

10 Make another 15 T blocks in the same way and then complete the quilt as explained on page 88, starting by adding the borders.

Fig 4c
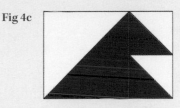

Fig 4d

Creative Options

The quilt stitching pattern doesn't have to be complicated, but it does provide an opportunity to build on the quilt's theme, to draw attention to certain patterning or to add another dimension in terms of texture or patterning. With a bit of ingenuity you can do all three.

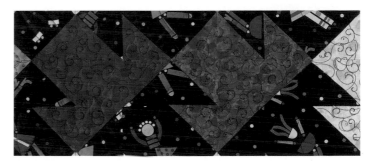

FOLK – DANCING (above) The themes of this quilt are movement and fun, so the quilting needed to enforce this. Swirling black stitching all over the brightly coloured background fabrics add movement and energy.

TEA TIME (left) Here's a good example of how the quilt stitches can build on the quilt's theme. On the yellow Ts I used matching thread to quilt tiny T shapes above each teacup and stipple quilt the rest.

Delectable Mountains

I found the design that inspired these quilts on the floor of the stunning cathedral in Siena, Tuscany. I had long been on the lookout for this design because it reminds me of Delectable Mountains with its undulating rectangles mirrored on the opposite side. It is usually seen as a border in just two rows of black and white so I was pleased to find it as an overall design.

Working out how to piece a tessellation without setting in seams can be difficult. When drafting this quilt I drew lines across the paper to create rows of strips. I cut out my fabrics and pieced them one by one in long rows, but after I had made three quilts this way I realized that I could piece more quickly if I redrew the design with a large central square and four small outer rectangles for each colour. This made the piecing process much quicker and it is this method that I share with you on pages 95–97.

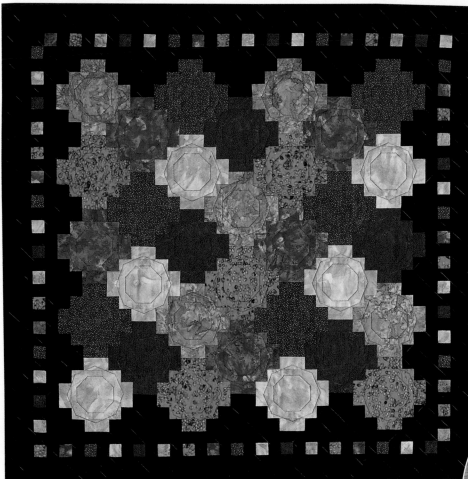

EVENING MOODS 38 x 38in
Quilted by Rosemary Archer

Evening Moods

I think it is vital to be open to change when designing a quilt. In this case, for example, I had originally chosen a colourful focus fabric to use in the border and found six matching fabrics in dark and light values of blue, green and red to go with it. Once they were laid out, I realized that the focus fabric made it all too confusing so I abandoned it! Black works well for the border because it brings out all the colours of the quilt. It is enhanced by the mosaic of small coloured squares interleaved with black, which make an unusual frame around the quilt to draw the eyes in.

The original tiles date from the 14th century or earlier and have become very worn with the passage of time. Nevertheless the tessellation is quite visible.

MEMORIES OF SIENA 38 x 48½in
Quilted by Rosemary Archer and Pauline Blazey

Memories of Siena

This was the first quilt I made in the Delectable Mountains series and accurately represents the inner part of the design I saw on the floor tiles. I especially like its clean lines and bold geometric design. I used several different pale greys and blacks to replicate the original floor tiles as far as possible, and framed the interior with black sashing. I was going to stop there but felt that the quilt needed something extra. I chose to add a traditional border design of black squares on point. The addition of the dark peach batik as a background sets off the spare look of the black and white interior, which is echoed in the cool grey binding.

The peach batik fabric of the border captures the look of marble and gives the quilt a colourful lift.

Fizzy Pop

FIZZY POP 32¼ x 37½in
Quilted by Rosemary Archer

The diagonal stripes of the sashing and binding, created by cutting the fabric on the bias, add colour and movement.

After Memories of Siena I wanted to work on something colourful. This time I joined the outlines together to create interlocking shapes for a completely different look. I chose bright colours to make the quilt 'sing' and placed them at random, trying not to repeat them too often. When repeating a fabric, I placed it as far from the original as possible. To tie the colours together I chose a bright pink stripe for the sashing and binding, which I cut on the bias to give a barber's pole effect. The bright lime green of the border echoes the greens in the middle of the quilt.

Sunrise, Sunset

SUNRISE, SUNSET 53¼ x 58¼in
Quilted by Rosemary Archer

The grading of colours
by tone as they travel
diagonally across the
quilt adds a subtle
textural quality.

Wanting to experiment with a diagonal design, and wishing to create a new look, I decided to work with just two colours here – yellows and purples – from the palest, through to medium tones and dark values. In some diagonals I went from dark to light from top to bottom, in others I started with medium through to light and back to medium or from medium through to dark and back again. The mitred border frames the design well with the two palest colours of lavender and cream on the top and right side, and the dark brown and purple on the bottom and left side.

Underwater World

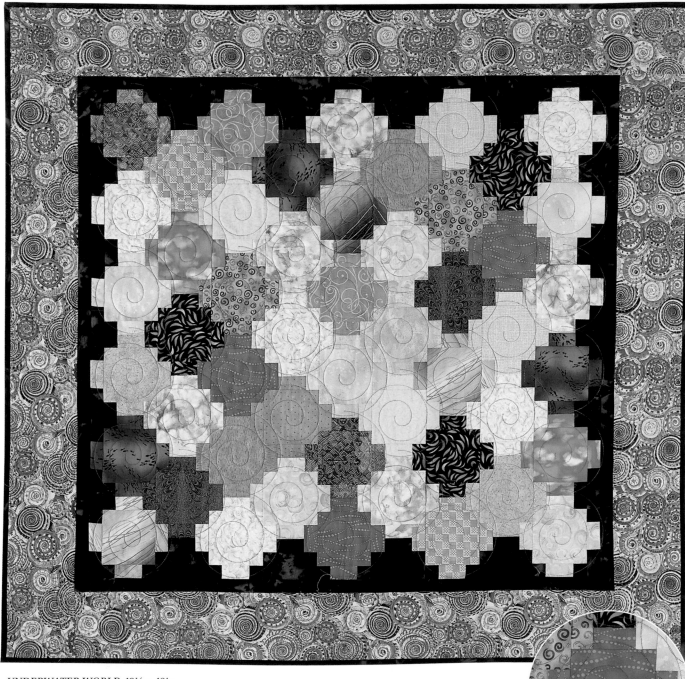

UNDERWATER WORLD 49½ x 48in
Quilted by Rosemary Archer

I found this border fabric in California while I was teaching there, and it immediately reminded me of sea snails. I chose it as my focus fabric and picked out most of the colours to go with it in the same shop. Many of the 23 fabrics I used twice and some three times. By now I had worked out a quick way of piecing the design. Dark turquoise blue at the edges brings the pattern to a close.

Swirling fabrics in greens, blues and turquoise capture the colour and excitement of the sea beneath the surface.

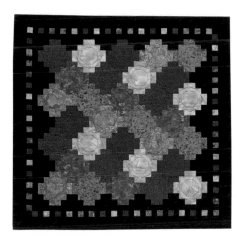

Quilt Size: 38 x 38in

MATERIALS

Fabric
100% cotton fabrics 44in wide:
• ¼ yard each of six contrasting fabrics (dark turquoise, pale green, red, pale turquoise, mid green, orange)
• 1 yard black

Batting
42in square

Backing
1⅛ yards of your choice

Rulers
2½ x 12½in
4½ x 12½in
4½ in square

Don't forget to...

✔ Use a design wall to help in the placement of the blocks. You can then stand back and judge the design before sewing, as you may wish to change some of the blocks around. (See Sewing Basics, page 10.)

Evening Moods

CUTTING

Measurements include ¼in seam allowances.

Dark turquoise and pale green
From each cut:
• 6 squares (4½in)
• 24 rectangles (2½ x 1½in)
• 1 strip (17 x 1½in) for the mosaic border

Red, pale turquoise, mid green and orange
From each cut:
• 5 squares (4½in)
• 20 rectangles (2½ x 1½in)
• 1 strip (17 x 1½in) for the mosaic border

Black
6 strips (44 x 1½in). Cut into:
  4 squares (1½in)
  18 rectangles (2½ x 1½in)
  14 rectangles (4½ x 1½in)
  6 rectangles (6½ x 1½in)
  2 strips (30¾ x 1½in) for border sashing
• 2 strips (32½ x 1½in) for border sashing
• 6 strips (17 x 1½in) for the mosaic border
• 2 strips (2½ x 34¾in) for border sashing
• 2 strips (2½ x 38½in) for border sashing
• 4 strips (44 x 2½in) for the binding

QUILT DESIGN

1 Place your six contrasting fabrics (4½in squares and 2½ x 1½in rectangles) into piles of each colour.
2 On the design wall place the first five colours as in **Fig. 1a**.
3 Now place the colours of the second row (**Fig 1b**).
4 Continue placing the fabrics in colour order in rows, using the photograph of the quilt as a guide.
5 Place the black rectangles (2½ x 1½in and 4½ x 1½in) in the outer spaces between the colours (**Fig 1c**).

Fig 1a

Fig 1b

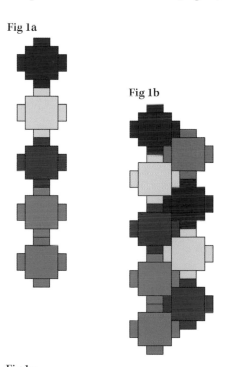

Fig 1c

To prevent distortion...

✔ When piecing rows together, sew the first three rows and then the last four rows, then join them together. This helps prevent distortion.

Fig 2a   **Fig 2b**

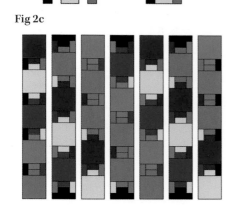

Fig 2c

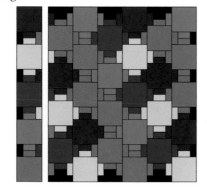

Fig 2d

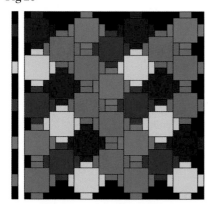

Fig 2e

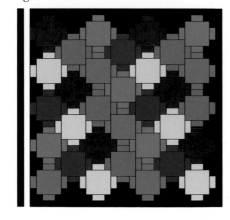

Fig 2f

BLOCK ASSEMBLY

Finished block size 6in square

1 Start by joining the 2½ x 1½in rectangles into blocks of four, as shown in **Figs 2a** and **2b**.

2 Press the seams towards the left (black section).

3 Join the pieced blocks to the 4½in squares in order (**Fig 2c**).

4 Join the rows together and the tessellation will suddenly become apparent (**Fig 2d**).

5 Now make the top and bottom strips as explained here. Referring to **Fig 2e** for the correct colour sequence, piece 2½ x 1½in coloured rectangles and 6½ x 1½in black rectangle together with a 1½in black square at each end. Each strip should be the width of the quilt. Attach the strips to the quilt.

6 In the same way piece together the two outer side strips using 2½ x 1½in coloured rectangles and 4½ x 1½in black rectangles with a 2½ x 1½in black rectangle at each end. Sew these on to the quilt (**Fig 2e**).

7 Attach one 30¾ x 1½in sashing strip to the top and bottom edges, and one 32½ x 1½in strip to the remaining two sides (**Fig 2f**).

8 Press the horizontal seams open. This makes the quilt lie flatter for quilting later on.

Outer Border

1 Referring to **Fig 3a**, take all the 17 x 1½in strips and lay them out in colour sequence starting with dark turquoise. Sew the strips together.

2 Press the coloured fabrics towards the black strips.

3 Cut this piece into 11 vertical strips 1½in wide (**Fig 3a**).

4 Join these eleven strips into one long strip, starting with dark turquoise.

Fig 3a

5 Count 32 squares and detach these from the long strip. Put this strip in place beside the right-hand side of the quilt.

6 Count 34 squares from the long strip, detach and place this strip next to the bottom of the quilt.

7 Repeat steps 5 and 6 to cut and position the strips for the top and left-hand side of the quilt.

8 Sew the shorter strips on to opposite sides of the quilt first, taking care to pin them carefully before sewing. They can stretch slightly, so use pins at both ends and in the middle and ease gently to fit as you pin the rest of the strip.

9 Attach the longer strips in the same way (**Fig 3b**).

10 Sew a 2½ x 34¾in black strip to the top and bottom of the quilt.

11 Sew a 2½ x 38½in black strip to each side, pressing the seams outwards. This completes the quilt.

Fig 3b

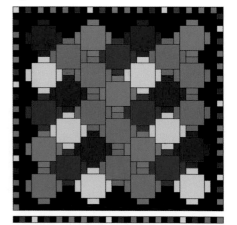

Quilting

1. Cut the backing fabric 2in larger all round than the quilt. Press any seams open.
2. Cut the batting/wadding to the same size.
3. Make the quilt sandwich of top, batting and backing and secure with safety pins, quilt tacks or basting spray if machine quilting, or by basting/tacking if hand sewing. (See Sewing Basics, page 16.)
4. Quilt as desired. This quilt was quilted with hexagons in the squares using variegated gold, orange and red rayon thread and with diagonal rectangles in the border area.

Binding and Finishing

1. Measure the perimeter of the quilt and join the 2½in black strips in a continuous strip to match your measurement.
2. Fold each strip in half along the length and press flat.
3. Refer to Sewing Basics, pages 17–19, for details on how to attach the binding, label and hanging sleeve.

Creative Options

The choice of thread colour for the quilting is very important and should add something extra to the finished effect. Sometimes the choice is easy, as for Memories of Siena, but when lots of colours are involved you may wish to use more than one thread or consider variegated thread, which is available in several different types and in lovely shimmering ranges.

MEMORIES OF SIENA The choice of thread colour was easy here – peach, to match the colour in the border. To counterbalance the angular design on the quilt, the stitching follows a simple but elegant curved line. This design looks rather like scrolling wrought-iron on a bannister or gate and so maintains the architectural theme of the quilt.

SUNRISE, SUNSET In keeping with the two colour theme of this quilt, two thread colours were used, each on their corresponding fabrics. The design also changes – stars on the yellow fabrics and flowers on the purple ones, with bold zigzags on the border. Straight stitching just inside the seams emphasizes the division between the diagonal bands of yellow and purple.

97

Eastern Promise

In the 1850s the industrialist Mr A. Maw toured mainland Europe to gather inspiration for making floor and wall tiles at Ironbridge in Shropshire, UK. One of his trips took him to Spain and the marvellous Alhambra Palace in Granada where he sketched and painted several tile designs, one of which is featured here. The original sketch is held in the archives at the Jackfield Tile Museum at Ironbridge. When I took a closer look, I could see that it was an intricate tessellating pattern, which after some study, I realized would split into square blocks, which I called Eastern Promise. Moorish Magic, opposite, resembles the original drawing.

FLORAL DANCE 46 x 46in
Quilted by Rosemary Archer

Floral Dance

My starting point for Floral Dance was the flowery fabric with a black background. I teamed it up with a super black fabric with pink dots and a co-ordinating green fabric with black dots. The design has two distinct blocks, which are mirror images of each other. Once the blocks were joined, I chose a bubble-gum pink with black dots for the sashing and turquoise fabric for the border, both of which link back to the colours of the floral fabric. The pink polka-dot binding repeats the sashing and completes this cheerful wall hanging. Instructions for making Floral Dance begin on page 103.

The inspirational
watercolour sketch.

MOORISH MAGIC 39 x 54in
Made by Judi Mendelssohn; quilted by Rosemary Archer

Moorish Magic

This quilt, made by Judi Mendelssohn, was inspired
directly by Mr Maw's original sketch made at the
Alhambra Palace. The fabrics are an almost exact match
of the colours and the border is an amalgam of the blue,
rust and cream of the inner quilt. The dark blue binding
frames the quilt well, echoing the dark blue shapes. I have
found, while making quilts inspired by tiles, that using
fabrics as close as possible in colour to the original tiles
always creates a special look and gives the feeling of being
drawn back to the roots of the original designer. This quilt
is made in 8in blocks.

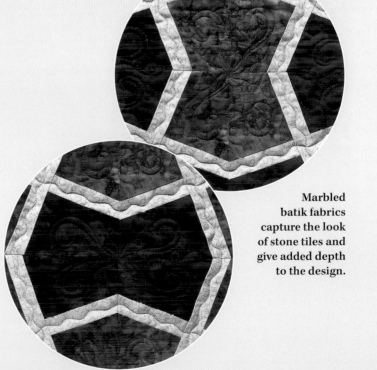

**Marbled
batik fabrics
capture the look
of stone tiles and
give added depth
to the design.**

Seville Surprise

SEVILLE SURPRISE 39 x 39in
Quilted by Rosemary Archer

I had been saving some poppy-red fabric for a special quilt and decided to use it here. I chose a very dark green check for the negative spaces, which picks up the dark green of the poppy fabric, and for the woven ribbons I found a really bright yellow that 'sings'. The mid green sashing harks back to the spotty background of the poppy fabric and ties in with the bright orange and yellow of the border. The dark green binding provides a neat frame and balances the dark green of the negative shapes. This quilt is made in 6in blocks.

A feathery design worked in variegated rayon thread embellishes every 'tile'.

Mardi Gras

MARDI GRAS 45½ x 45½in
Quilted by Rosemary Archer

In this quilt diagonal rows of several colours have two
interwoven ribbons of pink and dark turquoise running
through. Using the 6in block again, I put together groups of
fabrics that initially did not look as though they had much in
common. For the sashing I used the remains of the two ribbon
fabrics. The hand-dyed border fabric is exactly right and pulls
all the colours together. The binding is from the same piece
and I arranged it so that the colours of the border and the
binding contrasted, making a superb frame.

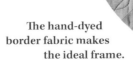

**The hand-dyed
border fabric makes
the ideal frame.**

Firebird

FIREBIRD 40 x 40in
Quilted by Rosemary Archer

Inspired by Stravinsky's ballet, this quilt was the last in this series. This time I redesigned the block, leaving out the woven ribbons. I chose twelve fabrics ranging from light yellow through the oranges and reds to deep dark brown to achieve the rich, sumptuous diagonal effect I was aiming for. Once I had pieced the blocks, it was very easy to press fusible black bias tape along the rows, which I secured with a zigzag stitch. The border brings all the colours together and the black sashing is echoed in the binding.

A dramatic fabric of spinning discs, used for the border, inspired the colours of this finale.

Quilt Size: 58½ x 47½in

MATERIALS

Fabric
100% cotton fabrics 44in wide:
- ¾ yard black
- ¾ yard green
- 1 yard floral
- ¾ yard pink
- ¾ yard turquoise

Batting
50 x 50in

Backing
2 yards your choice

Rulers and Templates
4½ x 12½in
6½in square
Template A1, A2 and A3

For quick cutting…

✔ You do not need to make templates B1, B2 and B3 if you fold the fabric when cutting and using the A templates, as you will be cutting mirror images.

Floral Dance

CUTTING

Measurements include ¼in seam allowances. See templates on page 104.

Black and green
5 strips (4⅛in wide). Fold each strip in half and cut 36 of template A1 to give 36 of A1 and 36 of B1

Floral
- 6 strips 1¼in wide. Fold each strip in half and cut 36 of template A2. This will give you 36 of A2 and 36 of B2
- 12 strips 1¼in wide. Fold each strip in half and cut 36 of template A3. This will give you 36 of A3 and 36 of B3
- 4 squares (4½in) for the border

Pink
- 4 strips (1½in wide). Cut into:
  2 strips (1½ x 36½in)
  2 strips (1½ x 38½in)
- 4 strips (2½in wide) for binding

Turquoise
4 strips (4½ x 38½in) for the border

Cutting the green and black fabrics.

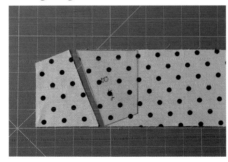

Cutting the floral fabrics.

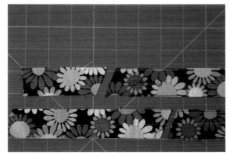

Don't forget to…

✔ Press the fabric before cutting. I use a fabric stabilizer or starch on the reverse side of the fabric. This makes for more accurate cutting, especially on long strips.

BLOCK ASSEMBLY

BLOCK A
Finished block size 6in square

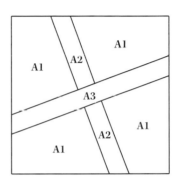

1 Sew a black A1 piece to the floral A2 strip. Sew a green A1 to the other side of the floral strip (**Fig 1a**).
2 Make a total of 36 of these units.
3 Sew 18 units to floral strips A3 (**Fig 1b**).
4 Join your two units together, as shown (**Fig 1c**).
5 Press each unit. You should have a total of 18 blocks.
6 Square up the blocks using a 6½in square ruler.

Fig 1a

Fig 1b

Fig 1c

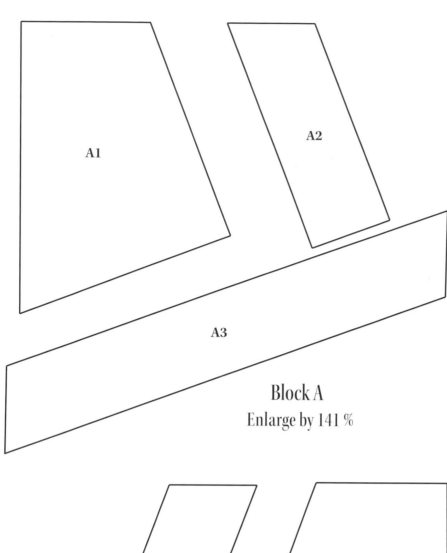

Block A
Enlarge by 141 %

A1

A2

A3

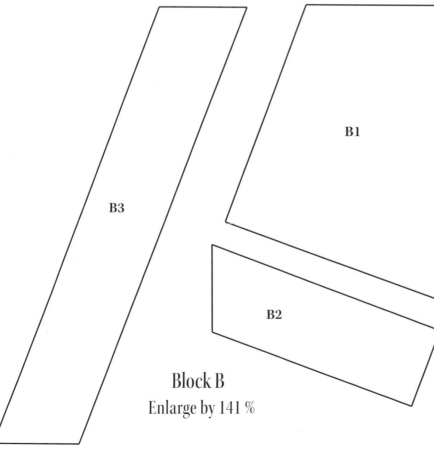

Block B
Enlarge by 141 %

B3

B1

B2

BLOCK B
Finished block size 6in square

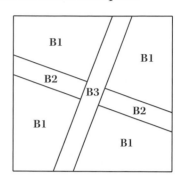

B1

B1

B2

B3

B2

B1

B1

1 Sew a black B1 piece to the floral B2 strip. Sew a green B1 to the other side of the floral strip (**Fig 2a**).
2 Make a total of 36 of these units.
3 Sew 18 units to floral strips B3 (**Fig 2b**).
4 Join your two units together, as shown (**Fig 2c**).
5 Press each unit. You should have a total of 18 blocks.
6 Square up the blocks using a 6½in square ruler.

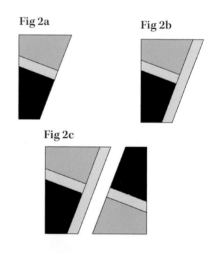

Fig 2a

Fig 2b

Fig 2c

Finished A and B blocks.

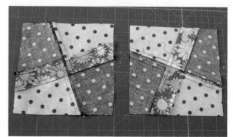

Squaring up the blocks.

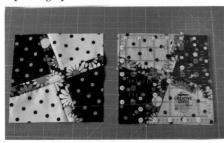

ASSEMBLING THE QUILT

1 Lay the blocks on the design wall, placing an A block in the top left hand corner, followed by a B block. Continue alternating the blocks in six rows of six (**Fig 5**).

2 Stand back to confirm that you have all the blocks in the correct positions.

3 Sew the horizontal rows together and press the seams of the rows in alternate directions.

4 Sew all the rows together, making sure that all the seams match correctly. Press the seams open to reduce bulk at the intersections.

5 Sew one 1½ x 36½in pink sashing strip to each side of the quilt. Press the seams outwards.

6 Sew one 1½in x 38½in pink sashing strip to the top and bottom of the quilt. Press the seams outwards.

Border

1 Sew a 4½in floral square to each end of two 4½ x 38½in turquoise border strips.

2 Sew the two remaining 38½ x 4½in turquoise strips to the sides of the quilt. Press the seams outwards.

3 Sew the turquoise and floral border strips to the top and bottom of the quilt (**Fig 6**).

Backing

1 Cut the backing fabric 2in larger all round than the quilt. Press any seams open.

2 Cut the batting/wadding to the same size.

Quilting

1 Make the quilt sandwich of top, batting and backing and secure with safety pins, quilt tacks or basting spray if machine quilting, or by basting/tacking if hand sewing. (See Sewing Basics, page 16.)

2 Quilt as desired. The inner part of Floral Dance was quilted with hearts and the floral woven ribbons were outlined. The border was quilted in a daisy-chain design to match the flowers on the ribbons.

Binding and Finishing

1 Measure the perimeter of the quilt and join the 2½in pink strips in a continuous piece to match your measurement.

2 Fold each strip in half along the length and press flat.

3 Refer to Sewing Basics, pages 17–19 for details on how to attach the binding, label and hanging sleeve.

For a flat finish…

✔ I carefully trim all the waste fabric at seam intersections to make the quilt lie flatter, which also makes it easier to quilt.

Fig 5

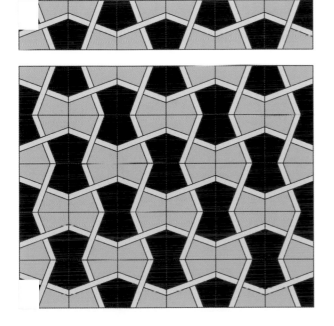

Fig 6

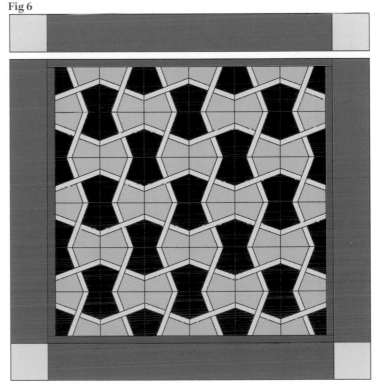

Gallery

I designed most of the quilts in this book, but it is always a good idea to see pieces made by as many quilt artists as possible to widen your horizons and make you aware of the wide range of possibilities. Here are six quilts inspired by tessellations that I hope will inspire you. All works are copyright in the name of the artist.

Dancing Triangles

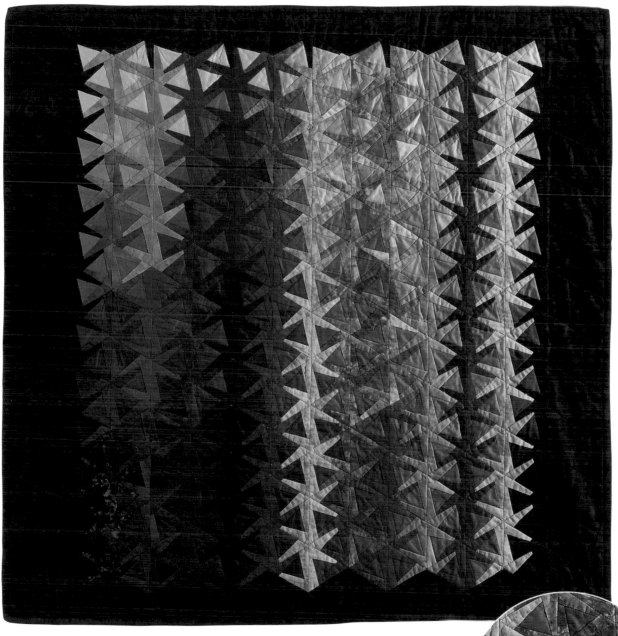

DANCING TRIANGLES 39½ x 39½in
Made by Khurshid Bamboat, UK

This design has been adapted from an article written by Gail
Garber. Using just one shape – the triangle – Khurshid explored
the effects achieved by tessellating the blocks to create a
myriad of stars. Khurshid has hand dyed most of the fabrics in
this piece and has successfully achieved a palette of graduated
vibrant colours. Each block was individually pieced on a
foundation and then machine quilted.

**By dying her own fabrics Khurshid was able
to begin the design process one stage earlier.**

Zigzags

ZIGZAGS 40 x 40in
Made by Tracey Brookshier, USA

Tracey made this quilt as part of a transatlantic quilt challenge, which specified that six out of eight challenge fabrics had to be used together with as many others as you desired. Tracey created this attractive and bold tessellated design by using the strip piecing method. Twenty-one combinations of three strips were sewn to give the effect of steps travelling diagonally across the quilt. The orange just inside the binding gives the effect of a double frame.

Colourful fabrics draw the eye and make this quilt 'sing'.

Calgary Heights to Downtown Vancouver

CALGARY HEIGHTS TO DOWNTOWN VANCOUVER 28 x 28in
Made by Christine Evans, UK

Chris produced this attractive quilt as a memento of a special trip she and her husband made to celebrate their ruby wedding anniversary touring Alberta and British Columbia that culminated at Vancouver Island. The Inner City design was adapted from a project by Mary Hewson, and Chris has added extra Tumbling Blocks at the top and the bottom of the quilt. Using a brilliant palette of fabrics, and shading the blocks in light, medium and dark values, Chris has created the illusion of a three-dimensional design. Her technique was to hand piece the blocks over papers, which she then sewed together and machine quilted.

Christine pieced this quilt by hand using the English piecing method.

Falling Colours

In this original design, Jan used a strip piecing technique to achieve a tessellated pattern within the colour ranges of brown, purple, green and blue. Jan's highly artistic use of light, medium and dark values has enabled her to create an illusion of colours falling as water across the surface of the quilt. The black fabric acts as a perfect foil to the vibrant colours of the quilt.

The careful placing of values gives this quilt a wonderful three-dimensional effect.

FALLING COLOURS 46 x 80in
Made by Jan Hassard, UK

Turbulence

TURBULENCE 31 x 27in
Made by Mary Underwood, USA

Mary used a Tumbling Blocks design to create
this unusual tessellation. The swirling blue fabric
framing the inner quilt gives the illusion of the wind
blowing and hurling some of the blocks out of the
picture and off the edge of the quilt. The outer frame
of four fabrics adds a contemporary touch to this
traditional pattern.

**The Tumbling
Blocks really are
tumbling as they
seemingly fall out
of the design.**

111

Pinwheel Bouquet

PINWHEEL BOUQUET 54 x 54in
Made by Darra Williamson, USA

The simple pattern of the Pinwheel block is used to good effect in Darra's quilt. The combination of 49 different fabrics, which represent summer flowers, is a wonderful example of a scrap quilt. Setting the square of fabrics on point and surrounding them with a patterned black background accentuates the tessellated shapes of the pinwheel. The dark pink border acts as an excellent frame for this pinwheel bouquet. Darra has quilted beautiful feathers by hand in the black background.

Hand quilting adds to the traditional look of this splendid piece.

Wingdings

WINGDINGS 57 x 57in
Made by Frances Cunningham, USA, quilted by Fay Collinsworth;
photograph by Christopher Dettweiler

This quilt was based on a pattern drafted by Karen Matsumoto, which she calls Flights of Imagination. Frances was interested in making a study of transparency to make the centre diamond appear to be three-dimensional. The individual diamond shapes, composed of two large and two small triangles, were assembled, and the quilt was pieced in diagonal rows. Frances designed the quilting pattern, which was quilted by Fay Collinsworth.

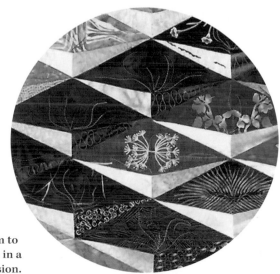

The diamonds seem to rise out towards us in a skilful piece of illusion.

Resource Library

There are many shapes that tessellate. This is just a small selection, which you can use as a resource. For each one, the outline is first given in black and white to show how the design is made up. I have then given a coloured illustration to demonstrate how a pattern will emerge in colour. The shapes divide into three basic groups for piecing. The first group is made up of square blocks as in Right-Angled Triangles, Autumn Leaves, Polygon Maze and Tulips. The second group are shapes that are suitable for strip piecing, for example Horizontal Rectangles, Tilted Rectangles, Inverted Arrows and Windmills. The third group is made up of shapes that are more complicated to piece, such as Split Diamonds, which can be pieced over papers and Winged Triangles, a split parallelogram that can be pieced in rows.

If you trace over the line drawings you can colour in the patterns to form different designs. You can then use these as inspiration for making a quilt with your favourite fabrics in your chosen colour-way. All these designs are in the public domaine.

Right-Angled Triangles

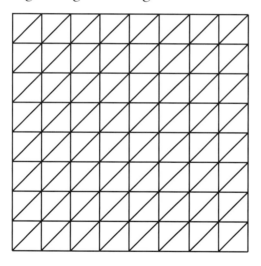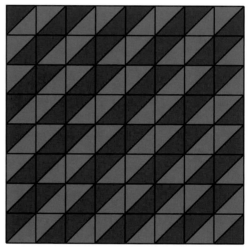

Autumn Leaves

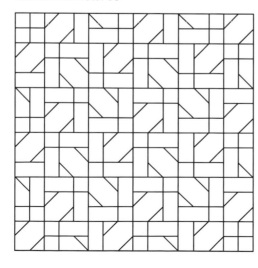

Polygon Maze

 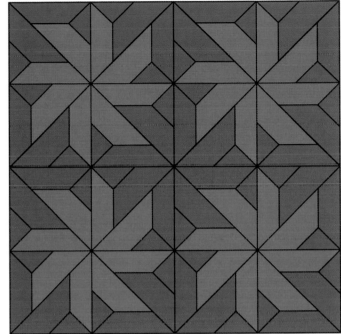

Tulips

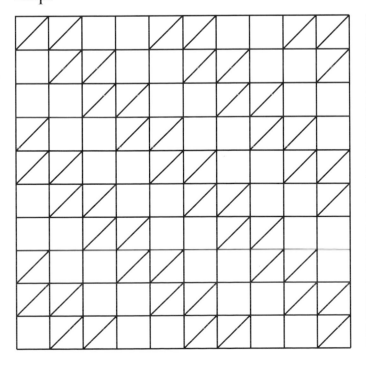 

Horizontal Rectangles

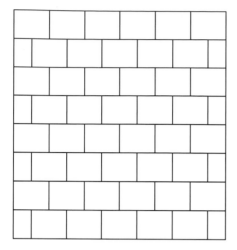  

Tilted Rectangles

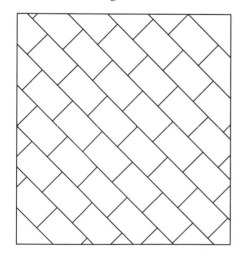 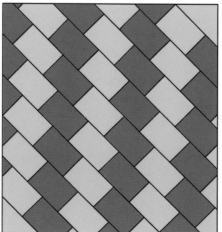 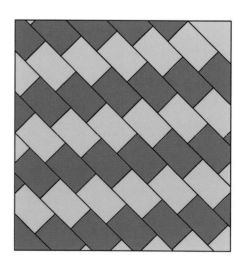

Inverted Arrows

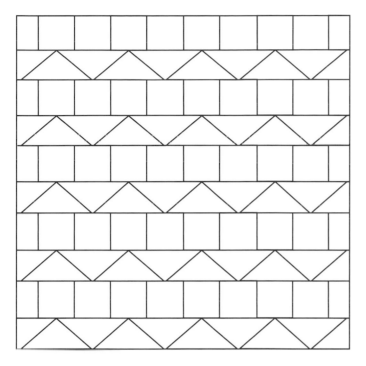
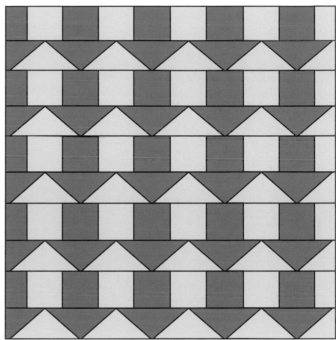

Windmills

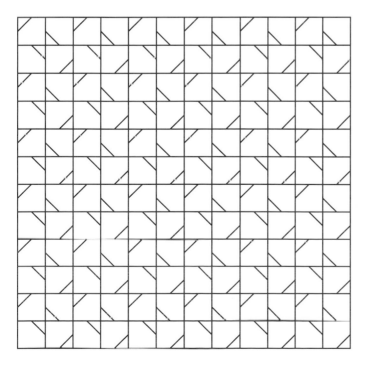

Winged Triangles

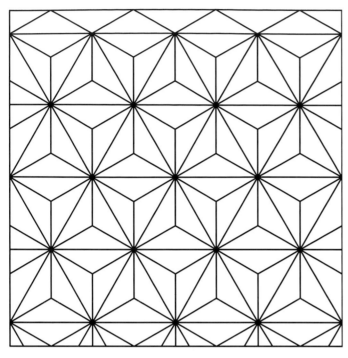 

Split Diamonds

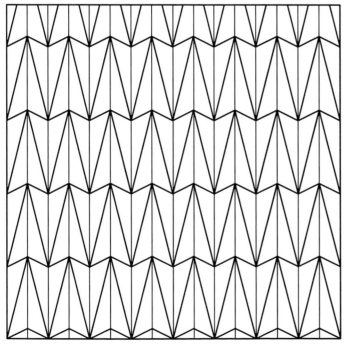 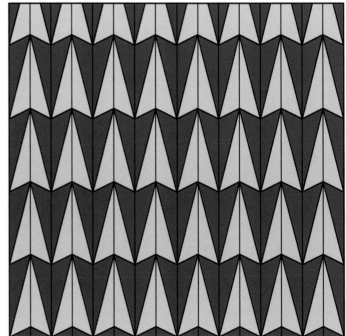

Acknowledgments

There are many people who have encouraged me in writing this book and although my name is at the top, this really is a team effort! I am truly grateful to all of them.

- Photography is one of the most important elements in any quilt book and I am so lucky to have a husband who has turned from being a lawyer into a professional photographer. Neil, thank you for being there for me all the time and for producing the beautiful illustrations.

- Ann Rhodes has translated my sketches and photographs into diagrams for the projects – her skill on the computer, her patience and thoughtfulness have been invaluable.

- Rosemary Archer is a highly talented and artistic long-arm quilter and I am so glad I live close to her. She has greatly enhanced my quilts with her beautiful and innovative designs.

- Good friends who give weekly encouragement and can hem bindings at the drop of a hat are few and far between. I am particularly grateful to Sally Ablett for her friendship and for keeping me on the straight and narrow and smiling throughout. Sally has contributed two quilts to this book. Many thanks also to Sharon Pederson for hemming so many bindings for me.

- Making so many quilts non stop unfortunately caused wear and tear on certain joints. I thank Mala Balani, my osteopath for her great healing powers and wonderful sense of humour, but I am not going to give up quilting for tap dancing!

- Particular thanks are due to the following:

- The team at David & Charles: Executive Editor Cheryl Brown for her quiet encouragement and belief in me, Editor Ame Verso, Project Editor Betsy Hosegood, Art Editor Prudence Rogers and Dianne Huck for the final technical checks.

- Creative Grids who have been most generous with their excellent rulers and who have helped me to develop the Diamond Template.

- Judi Mendelssohn and Tracey Brookshier who made a quilt each especially for the project chapters and Pauline Blazey who quilted two of my quilts.

- Khurshid Bamboat, Tracey Brookshier, Frances Cunningham, Chris Evans, Jan Hassard, Mary Underwood and Darra Williamson, all of whom contributed to the Gallery section (pages 106–113).

- Mike Harris of VSM for introducing me to the Husqvarna Viking SE sewing machine.

- Bryan Taphouse of Perfect Occasions and Maggie Rowell and Sharon Wood, freelance fabric designers for Moda for supplying fabric.

- Numerous quilt shops of Great Britain and the United States for encouraging me to build up my collection of fabrics.

About the Author

Christine Porter has been a quilter for 15 years. She is a highly respected and experienced teacher who not only lectures and judges throughout Britain and the United States but who has also won awards for her quilts in both countries. Her special field of interest is translating floor-tile designs into quilts, a subject she covered extensively in her first book for David & Charles, *Quilt Designs from Decorative Floor Tiles*, and she particularly enjoys creating a contemporary look through her use of colour and fabric style.

Until recently, Christine was for many years co-editor of Britain's leading patchwork magazine, *Patchwork & Quilting*. In addition Christine is director of her own company, Cabot Quilting Conferences, which brings top international quilters to Britain to teach in luxury hotels, to share their skills with other quilters from around the world. Christine has appeared on America's HGTVs series 'Simply Quilts' hosted by Alex Anderson and has been a Fabric Design Consultant for the Woodrow Studios in the UK.

Christine lives in Bristol, UK, with her husband Neil and black labrador, Rosie.

For more of Christine's work and details of her workshops and quilting conferences visit: **www.christineporterquilts.com**

Bibliography

DAY LEWIS F.
Pattern Design
(Dover Publications Inc. 1999)
ISBN 0-486-40709-8

HORNUNG CLARENCE P.
Geometric Patterns and How to
Create Them
(Dover Publications Inc. 2001)
ISBN 0-486-41733-6

SEYMOUR DALE &
BRITTON JILL
Introduction to Tessellations
(Dale Seymour Publications 1989)
ISBN 0-86651-461-9

ROBINSON JACKIE
Tessellations
Animas Quilts Publishing
ISBN 1-885156-03-0

Useful Addresses

UK

Busy Bees
The Craft Units, Tredegar House,
Newport, Gwent NP10 8YW
Email: busybeespatchwork@
hotmail.com

The Contented Cat & Rio Designs
Flint Cottage, Treacle Lane, Rushden,
Buntingford, Hertfordshire SG9 0SL
www.contentedcat.co.uk
www.riodesigns.co.uk

The Cotton Patch
1285 Stratford Road, Hall Green,
Birmingham, West Midlands B28 9AJ
www.cottonpatch.co.uk

**Creative Grids (Rulers, Triangle and
Diamond templates)**
Unit 5 Swannington Road, Cottage
Lane Industrial Estate, Broughton
Astley,
Leicestershire LE9 6TU
www.creativegrids.com

Creative Quilting
32 Bridge Road, East Molesey,
Surrey
KT8 9EU
Tel: 0208 941 7075
www.creativequilting.co.uk

Frome Valley Quilting
Rosemary Archer, 335 Church Road,
Frampton Cottrell, Bristol BS36 2AB
www.fromevalleyquilting.co.uk

Hannah's Room
50 Church Street, Brierley, Barnsley,
South Yorkshire S72 9HT
www.hannahsroom.co.uk

Husqvarna Viking Sewing Machines
VSM United Kingdom, Ravensbank
House,
Ravensbank Drive, North Moons Moat,
Redditch, Worcestershire B98 9NA
www.husqvarnaviking.com

Perfect Occasions
Bombay House, Shearbridge Road,
Bradford BD7 1NX
Email: btaphouse@aol.com

The Quilt Room
20 West Street, Dorking,
Surrey RH4 1BL
www.quiltroom.co.uk

Stitch in Time
293 Sandycombe Road, Kew,
London TW9 3LU
www.stitchintimeuk.com

USA

Animas Quilts Publishing
(Binding Mitre Tool)
830 Douglas Hill Road,
Eureka, MT 59917
www.animas.com

Come Quilt with Me
(Diamond template in USA)
3903 Avenue 1, Brooklyn,
NY 11210
www.comequiltwithme.com

The Cotton Patch
1025 Brown Ave, Lafayette,
CA 94549
www.cottonpatch@quiltusa.com

The Quilt Scene
8785 SW 132nd St, Miami,
FL 33176
www.quiltscene.com

The Stitchin' Post
PO Box 280, 311 West Cascade Street,
Sisters, OR 97759
www.stitchinpost.com

Index